PHYSICIANS
AND WAR

First published in Great Britain in 2016 by Little, Brown

Copyright © Royal College of Physicians 2016

The moral right of the authors has been asserted.

All images from RCP collections unless otherwise indicated.

Designed by Emil Dacanay and Sian Rance, D.R. ink

A CIP catalogue record for this book is available from the British Library.

ISBN 978-1-4087-0628-2

Printed in China

COVER: *Gassed*. John Singer Sargent 1918 (© Imperial War Museum (ART 1460))
ENDPAPERS: *The meeting of Wellington and Blücher after Waterloo*. Daniel Maclise 1858 (© Royal Academy of Arts, London; Photographer: Prudence Cuming Associates Ltd)
PAGE 1: *The 8th Hussars on patrol* – Boer War. Photo Col Philip Stock
OPPOSITE: Army blood transfusion service – Fiji (© Imperial War Museum (NZ 1445))

500
REFLECTIONS
ON THE RCP
1518–2018

PHYSICIANS
AND WAR

Humphrey Hodgson
Simon Shorvon

Royal College
of Physicians

FOREWORD

The Royal College of Physicians was founded, by Royal Charter, in 1518 by King Henry VIII. Few professional organisations have been in continuous existence for so long, and over its five-hundred-year history the College has been at the centre of many aspects of medical life. Currently, the College has over thirty thousand members and fellows worldwide.

Its principal purpose is to promote the highest standards of medical practice in order to improve health and healthcare, and its varied work in the field is held in high regard. Over the years it has also accumulated a distinguished library, extensive archives, and a collection of portraits and other treasures, and has been housed in a number of notable buildings. As part of its quincentennial commemoration, a series of ten books has been commissioned. Each book features fifty reflections, thereby making a total of five hundred, intended to be a meditation on, and an exploration of, aspects of the College's work and its collections over its five hundred-year history.

In this, the fourth volume of the series, we turn to the dark topic of war for the fifty reflections. War has been a frequent feature of British life over the five hundred years of the College's existence, and has had an important place in the histories of both the College and medicine. This book provides a very brief survey of some aspects of this complex subject, and focuses upon the effects of war on medicine, and of medicine on war, from the perspective of the College and its members and fellows.

I would like to express my thanks for the enormous assistance provided in the acquisition of the images in this volume from Ms Julie Beckwith, head of the Library Services at the College and her colleagues Mr Peter Basham, Mr Stephen Deed and Ms Pamela Forde, and also to Dr Natalie Wilder, Ms Claire Daley and Mr Odhran O'Donoghue at the College and Ms Sian Rance the book designer, for their work in making the volume what it is, and also to our publisher Little, Brown. The help kindly provided by Dr Andrew Bamji in identifying World War I images is gratefully acknowledged.

Simon Shorvon -

Simon Shorvon, Harveian Librarian, Royal College of Physicians
Series Editor

CONTENTS

INTRODUCTION

The Royal College of Physicians has three elements: the Institution, its buildings and its people – fellows, members and licentiates. Over the five centuries since 1518 war has impacted on each of these. This book illustrates some of the many ways in which that occurred, from the political to the personal, from the national role of the College to individual experiences in battle.

A further thread running through the book is the interplay between war and the science and practice of medicine. War creates new diseases, results in innovation and medical advances, and stimulates new approaches to the organisation of care. As Wilmot Herringham, First Consultant Physician to the Army in the First World War, and one of Britain's and the College's resolute military doctors wrote:

> *The War has shown the immense services which original research can render to preserve the efficiency of an army ... results could be obtained by the union of clinical and pathological research, not only at home, but also in the actual area of military operations ... clinical medicine and surgery in war time is not of necessity rough in method and imperfect in attainment; but is susceptible of a high and exquisite perfection and affords scope for the finest scientific work.*

The authors have drawn on the College's archives as well as other sources and have also taken the liberty of highlighting wartime records of individual doctors. One may reflect that the contribution of College fellows to the advance of medicine in periods of war, and to caring for the injured of war, has been strikingly great in proportion to their small number. When the Battle of Sedgemoor took place (1685) the total complement of fellows was only forty-five, rising to fifty-three at Trafalgar (1805), and seventy-two at the time of Waterloo (1815). At Balaclava (1854), fellowship stood at 181, and was at 304 when the siege of Mafeking was raised (1900). When World War I broke out there were only 352 fellows, and 598 at the start of World War II (now the College has over 16,000 fellows). So, much was accomplished by very few.

Further, the authors apologise that, for every individual whose biography or contribution we have mentioned, there are far more whom we have omitted. Our only excuse is that this short book is essentially a brief and impressionistic glance at a large and complex topic.

Finally, as the volume is one of a series which is a celebration of 500 years of the College, we have to a great extent avoided dwelling on the horrors of, as Wilfred Owen said, 'the pity of war'. To the most serious-minded of our readers we apologise and seek forbearance, but above all doctors deal with, and are, people, and it is their humanity, which plays a role in the history of all conflicts, that is our perspective.

OPPOSITE: Bomb-damaged library, Royal College of Physicians, Pall Mall, November 1940

THE TURBULENT SEVENTEENTH CENTURY

The political changes during the seventeenth century were arguably the most profound of the 500 years of the College's existence. The *de facto* union with Scotland was ushered in at the accession of King James I; the growing rift between Charles I and Parliament led to the dissolution of Parliament in 1629; civil war broke out in 1642; the King was executed in 1649; Cromwell's Protectorate lasted for twelve years until the Restoration of Charles II in 1660, who was succeeded for a short-lived reign by his Catholic brother James II. James saw off the Protestant rebellion by the Duke of Monmouth at Sedgemoor, but was deposed by the Glorious Revolution of 1688 which brought William of Orange and Queen Mary to the throne.

THE COLLEGE BEFORE AND DURING THE CIVIL WAR

Charles I had not endeared himself to the College. His levies to support wars with France and Spain, and his support for the Church of England as a body able to license physicians, were scarcely popular – the response of the College was to deny its own licences to anyone in holy orders. However, both before and during the Civil War, the College – at that time a select body of only thirty-five fellows – remained neutral. As time passed, however, the development of London as a parliamentary stronghold dictated the views it espoused. Indeed in 1643 the College 'volunteered' three of its fellows to serve in a medical capacity in the parliamentary army.

ABOVE: King Charles I
OPPOSITE: Untitled allegory for the English Civil War, taken from *A true copy of the journal of the High Court of Justice for the tryal of Charles I...* John Nalson, published London, 1684. Note the carriage of state commandeered by the Devil, and the beheaded King Charles crushed beneath its wheels. NB The image has been reversed.
(All photography Mike Fear)

 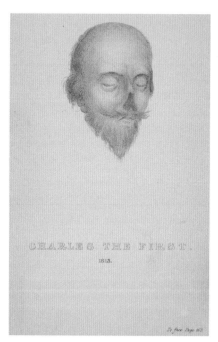

ABOVE LEFT: The trial of the King. Illustration taken from *A true copy of the journal of the High Court of Justice for the tryal of Charles I.* John Nalson, published London, 1684
ABOVE RIGHT: Charles I's head pictured after exhumation from *An account of the opening of the tomb of King Charles I.* Sir Henry Halford, published London, 1831
OPPOSITE: Frontispiece taken from *A true copy of the journal of the High Court of Justice for the tryal of Charles I.* John Nalson, published London 1684
(All photography Mike Fear)

Individuals who were Royalists were left in a difficult position. Prior to the war fellows had often been, as would be expected, physicians to the royal family and the Court. Some of the more adaptable rapidly moved to provide services to the parliamentary faction as times changed. While the College's political stance remained neutral (or flexible), different individuals supported one or other side or, in the case of some enterprising fellows, different sides at different times.

Charles I was tried in 1649 and executed on 30 January, walking out from the first floor of what is now the Banqueting House in Whitehall. Not wishing to inconvenience the executioner (or perhaps to ensure he would be efficiently dispatched), he is said to have asked the axe-man 'Does my hair trouble you?'.

Two hundred years later, Sir Henry Halford (1766–1844; PRCP 1820–44; FRS) was present when an unmarked coffin was opened in Henry VIII's vault. The head of the executed King, according to Halford, was preserved sufficiently for the resemblance to his portraits to be discerned. Bizarrely, Halford is said to have taken a piece of vertebra showing the mark of the axe as a subject for after-dinner conversation.

A

TRUE COPY

OF THE

JOURNAL

OF

𝔗𝔥𝔢 𝔥𝔦𝔤𝔥 𝔠𝔬𝔲𝔯𝔱 𝔬𝔣 𝔍𝔲𝔰𝔱𝔦𝔠𝔢,

FOR THE

TRYAL

OF

K. CHARLES I.

As it was Read in the

House of Commons,

AND

Attested under the hand of PHELPS,
Clerk to that Infamous Court.

Taken by *J. NALSON*, LL D. *Jan.* 4. 1683.

With a Large Introduction.

LONDON,

Printed by *H. C.* for *Thomas Dring*, at the *Harrow* at
the Corner of *Chancery-Lane* in *Fleet-street*, 1684.

Cromwell's Protectorate purged London of Royalists. William Harvey (1578–1657; FRCP 1607) had been expelled under a proclamation for removing all Papists, all officers and soldiers of fortune, and 'divers other delinquents' from London and Westminster. The College sought to bolster its position by requesting and obtaining letters patent from Cromwell 'Oliver Lord Protector', confirming the rights and privileges granted by Henry VIII in 1518.

TOP: Letters patent of Oliver Lord Protector, 18 December 1657, confirming the College's privileges
ABOVE: Cromwell's *proclamation commanding all persons...of the late kings party... to depart out of... London.* Published London, 6 July 1655
(All photography Mike Fear)

At the restoration of Charles II in 1660 the College, at an extraordinary Comitia meeting waxed enthusiastic and unequivocal: 'When for about twenty years now (when dissolution and idleness had put an end to good manners) some seditious "tribunes" of the people and ill-conditioned scoundrels had defiled all things … the Phoenix … rose at last'!

The King granted a new charter to the College in the name of 'Kings College of Physitians in the Cittie of London'. One advantage of the King's patronage was that: 'every Physitian, who is or shall be a member of our said Colledge be free, and exempt, and discharged of and from all watch and ward, and of and from bearing and providing armes …' – though it appears the College had to pay £150 for this privilege.

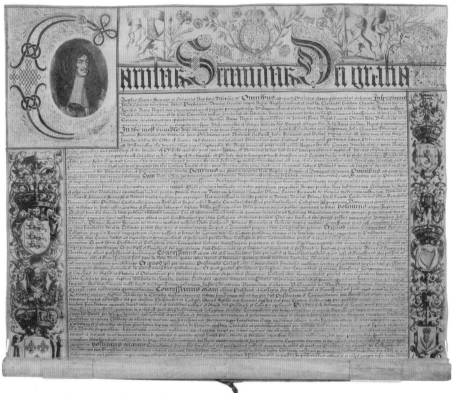

King Charles II's new charter for the College,
27 February 1673 (Photography Mike Fear)

THE LETANY

OF

JOHN BASTWICK,

Doctor of Phisicke,

Being now full of Devotion, as well in respect of the common calamities of plague and pestilence ; as also of his owne patticular miserie : lying at this instant in *Limbo Patrum.* Set downe in two Letters to Mr. *Aquila Wykes,* keeper of the Gatehouse, his good Angell.

IN WHICH

There is an universall challenge to the vvhole World, to prove the parity of Ministers, to be *jure divino.*

ALSO

A full demonstration, that the Bishops are neither Christs, nor the Apostle Successors, but enemies of *Christ* and his *Kingdome,* and of the *Kings most excellent Majesties prerogative Royall.*

All which hee undertaketh to make good before King and Counsell, with the hazard of otherwise being made a prey to their insatiable indignation.

A Booke very usefull, and profitable for all good Christians to read, for the stirring up of devotion in them likewise.

PROVERB. Chap. 25. verf. 2.
It is the glory of God to conceale a thing, but the honour of the King is to search out a matter.

PRINTED

By the speciall procurement, and for the especiall use of our English Prela in the yeare of Remembrance, *Anno* 1 6 3 7.

SOME WARRING FELLOWS

One victim of the Catholic leanings of Charles I was John Bastwick (1593–1654; LRCP 1627), a licentiate of the College. He was:

... apparently not satisfied with his progress in the profession, and being a man of strong zeal and warm imagination, he applied himself to writing, more particularly against Popery ... The bishops of the Church of England conceiving themselves calumniated, our author was brought before the High Commission Court, and on the 12th February, 1633, was fined 1,000l, sentenced to be excommunicated, debarred the practice of physic, his books to be burnt, to pay the costs of suit, and to remain in prison until he made his recantation ...

The College was sufficiently compliant to carry out its part of the sentence and revoked his licence to practice.

During his confinement Bastwick wrote *Letany*, 'wherein he grossly reflected on the bishops, taxed them with an inclination to Popery'. In 1637, information was exhibited against him and two others for 'writing and publishing seditious, schismatical, and libellous books against the hierarchy and the Church'. The defendants were censured as 'scandalous, seditious, and infamous persons, and condemned in a fine of 500l each, to stand in the pillory, and there to lose their ears, and to perpetual imprisonment in three remote places of the kingdom'.

All these punishments were exacted, though generally considered exorbitant and disproportionate. After Parliament was restored in 1640, a petition was presented to the House of Commons 'wherein it was requested that the justice and rigour of their sentence might be reviewed and considered'.

The House of Commons declared that the proceedings against Bastwick were illegal, unjust and against the liberty of the subject; that the sentence passed upon him be rescinded, his fine remitted and he himself be restored to his profession; and that for reparation, he ought to have 5,000l out of the estates of the Archbishop of Canterbury, the High Commissioners and those lords who had voted against him in the Star Chamber.

ABOVE: Portrait of John Bastwick as Captain of a 'Foote Company'
OPPOSITE: Title page to *The letany of John Bastwick, doctor of phisicke... John Bastwick,* published London, 1637
(All photography Mike Fear)

William Harvey (1578–1657). Engraving by J. Houbraken after W.V. Bemmel, 1739 (Photography Mike Fear)

The College of Physicians, compliant again, reinstated him as a licentiate, but the confusion of the times is said to have prevented the payment of the 5,000*l.* Subsequently he worked with the parliamentary army, but was captured and imprisoned for two years by the Royalists.

The most famous royal sympathiser was William Harvey, physician to Charles I; indeed he accompanied the King when he left London in 1642, and was present at the battle of Edgehill, during which he was left in charge of the King's sons. During the battle 'he withdrew with them under a hedge, and tooke out of his pocket a booke and read; but he had not read very long before a bullet of a great gun grazed on the ground neare him, which made him remove his station'. While

away from London, Harvey's lodgings were looted and his manuscript on insect reproduction stolen: 'Of all the losses he sustained no greife was so crucifying to him as the losse of these papers, which for love or money he could neither retrieve or obtaine'. When the College elected as President Dr John Clarke (?–1653), a staunch parliamentarian, Harvey refused to enter the College whilst Clarke was in the chair.

Other Royalists were more malleable. George Bate (1609–69; FRCP 1640; FRS) was the King's chief physician in Oxford in 1642, but as the tide of the struggle changed he returned to London. Although he wrote 'the regall apology' defending the King against the House of Commons – 'Blush, O England! For these thy sons whose Impudence hath forgot all bounds' – he was versatile enough not only to become Cromwell's personal physician, but also (to the resentment of his colleagues) to be the first physician appointed by Charles II at the Restoration. Bate's popularity with the King is said to reflect a report that he had hastened Cromwell's death with poison. Not for nothing was he described as 'the amphibious and ambidextrous Dr Bate'.

One of those who resented Bate's preferment was Baldwin Hamey (1600–76; FRCP 1633/4), who exploited the troubles of the times not apparently for personal gain but for the College's. In 1644 he (and most of the fellows), subscribed to the Solemn League and Covenant, an agreement between the Scots and most English Parliamentarians to support Protestantism and extirp popery. He could therefore exploit the

ABOVE LEFT: Baldwin Hamey (1600–76). Portrait by Matthew Snelling 1674 (Photography Mike Fear)
ABOVE RIGHT: Memorial to Dr William Oliver, Bath, Somerset (© Liquid Light / Alamy Stock Photo)

confiscation of church property ordered by Parliament and buy the lease of the land upon which the College stood – Amen Corner – which he then gifted to the College. However, Hamey also sent money to the exiled Charles II and presented him at the restoration with a diamond ring from Charles I's effects 'bought from the Rebel's hand' for £500. Endearingly, when required to 'go to hear what he hated – a barber or a cobbler hold forth; he always took care that his servant should carry for him … an edition of Virgil … resembling an Octavo bible, to entertain himself'.

The avowed Catholicism of James II, in contrast to the less obvious sympathies of Charles II, led to armed insurrection. The Duke of Monmouth's Protestant rebellion came to an end at the Battle of Sedgemoor, 1685. William Oliver (1659–1716; LRCP 1692; FRS) later fought with Monmouth and escaped the battle, thus avoiding trial and assured execution at the Bloody Assizes. He perfected his career in Bath as the inventor of the Bath Oliver biscuit.

Less fortunate was Benjamin Temple (?–1685; LRCP 1677), a licentiate of the College, who was on his way to Holland to improve himself in his profession when he met with the Duke of Monmouth, who engaged him as his physician and surgeon in an expedition intended, so he was told, to seize some of the West Indian islands. Apparently he knew nothing of the Duke's 'treasonable design of invading England' till they had been some time at sea. He was 'taken prisoner at Sedgemoor, tried at Dorchester in September, and being found guilty was sentenced to be executed, with eleven others, near the spot where Monmouth had landed'.

van Trompe going about to please his masters, ships a sea, getting a good wetting. J.M.W. Turner 1844 (Digital image courtesy of the Getty's Open Content Program)

NAVAL MATTERS

Sedgemoor is stated to be the last battle on English soil. The involvement of the College with war continued, however, with battles overseas or at sea.

The Dutch and the English fought three naval wars during the seventeenth century, commencing during the parliamentary era, and these presented a novel problem as the wounded from sea battles up and down the Channel and off the east coast were landed at many scattered ports. The Admiralty turned to the colourful Daniel Whistler (1619–84; PRCP 1683–84), a graduate of Leyden, and incidentally author of *De Morbo puerili Anglorum, quem patrio idiomate indigenae vocant "The Rickets".* He played a significant role in organising on-shore naval hospitals during a crisis precipitated by the Admiralty's responsibilities for over 300 sick and wounded sailors in Portsmouth after the battle of Portland in 1643. The Navy had run up a bill of more than £600 over the course of three weeks in Portsmouth and Gosport to pay for care for wounded seamen. Whistler thereafter advised the Lords of the Admiralty for several decades – he maintained that moving sick sailors inland was the best cure for the navy's sick. Interestingly, the College's memoir of him in William Munk's 'Roll of the Royal College of Physicians' makes no mention of this, but comments plangently upon his character, even though he later became President of the College:

ABOVE LEFT: Daniel Whistler (1619–84). Artist unknown
ABOVE RIGHT: William Cockburn (1669–1739). Engraving by Robert White
(All photography Mike Fear)

'Dr Whistler's character will not bear examination: and it would have been well for the College had he not been admitted to some at least of the places of trust he was elected to fulfil … there is a portrait in the College in company too good for his deserts.'

A separate parliamentary request involved another of the College's fellows in naval matters. Paul de Laune (?–1655; FRCP 1618) was one of three fellows recommended to Parliament and he became Physician General to the Fleet under Cromwell in 1654. He voyaged to the West Indies at the time of the capture of Jamaica in 1655, where he is believed to have perished.

In the late seventeenth century another figure from the College, William Cockburn (1669–1739; LRCP 1694), became physician to the Fleet. He published *The Nature and Cure of the Distempers that are incident to Seafaring People, with Observations on the Diet of Seamen in H.M. Navy*. Indeed he persuaded the Admiralty to conduct a sea trial of his anti-dysentery remedy. He also achieved the reputation of being 'an eminent physician, immensely rich', and was Jonathan Swift's doctor; but was subjected to ridicule when he proposed to an aristocratic lady with the words, 'if an old man and £50,000 can be acceptable to you'. She did not long demur.

ABOVE: Robert Jenkin displaying his ear to Parliament 1738 – notably seven years after being separated from it (©The Trustees of the British Museum. All rights reserved)

THE WAR OF JENKINS' EAR – A NAVAL POSTSCRIPT FROM THE EIGHTEENTH CENTURY

In 1731 officers of the Spanish *guardacostas* from the *La Isabela* boarded a British merchantman (and smuggler), the *Rebecca,* off the coast of Florida. In the ensuing altercation the Spanish commander cut off the ear of Captain Robert Jenkins. The repercussions festered for several years, among a multitude of trade and treaty disputes, but the loss of the ear (the ear itself being shown to Parliament in 1738) was one of the catalysts for a seven-year war with Spain. At one time it appeared that France might be drawn in, and the Admiralty sought the advice of the College on a number of matters. One was whether spirit distilled from English malt would be a suitable substitute for French brandy should the latter become unavailable. The College replied that – if of equivalent strength – the English liquor could appropriately be used to victual the Navy. The College also advocated spirit of vitriol (sulphuric acid) as a suitable treatment for scurvy, but did not commit itself as to dosage.

PAGES OVERLEAF: *The Scottish doctors march on the College in Warwick Lane 1767.* John June, published by Robert Sayer (Photography Mike Fear)

Invasion of the Council of the College of Physicians by the Scots doctors 1767. Artist unknown (Wellcome Library, London)

A BRAWL BUT NOT A WAR . . .

The College had its own internal wars. A longstanding feud between its fellows and licentiates flared up in 1767: a battle over the rights and spoils of practice in which birth, education and religion played a crucial role. Fellowship of the College was restricted to doctors with doctorates from Oxford or Cambridge only, and foreigners, Roman Catholics, dissenters, surgeons, apothecaries and others were excluded. The Scottish licentiates felt particularly bitter about this inequity, self-interest and restrictive practice, and in their ranks were worthy and celebrated doctors who were barred and excluded from College office. Several court cases took place over several years, but in each litigation failed. Matters reached boiling point in September 1767 when a group of licentiates marched on the College (housed then in Warwick Lane), broke down its doors and disrupted the meeting of the College Council. 'With inhuman violence they broke into this very senate, like swimming sea monsters in our medical ocean' was how the episode was described by Sir William Browne (1692–1774; PRCP 1765–67; FRS), the then College President, whose verse about Scottish graduates was equally contemptuous:

Scots Doctors, by a Hoggish sense, will root through any filth for pence
And if they can but gather fees, will spit upon Hippocrates.

The 'Siege of Warwick Lane Castle' caused much public amusement, and satirists and cartoonists had a field day. The rules of restrictive practice, though, were thenceforward slowly relaxed and the College survived to fight another day.

NAPOLEONIC WARS AND THE LATER NINETEENTH CENTURY

At the dawn of the nineteenth century Britain was, as was often the case in the previous 700 years, pitted in war against her ancient rival France. The French Revolutionary and Napoleonic Wars, as they have become known, had been declared against France in 1793, following the execution of Louis XVI, and skirmishes were had around the world against French forces. Then, after a brief truce in 1802–3, Britain declared war again and engaged in a series of battles which became a tussle between two military geniuses – Napoleon Bonaparte and the Duke of Wellington – including the Peninsular Wars, and culminating in the Battle of Waterloo in June 1815.

During this period military physicians began to come into their own. Granted, from the point of view of 'therapy', it was only the actions of the surgeons which really influenced survival and recovery, and the medical treatments of the physicians were largely useless. Furthermore, physicians were often despised and widely considered too intellectual and effete to be much use on the battlefield – in contrast to the military surgeons, men of action and of steel. Nevertheless, there were impressive advances in medical diagnosis, and from the point of view of organisation and structure of military medical facilities, it was the physicians who, during this period, made a mark.

The medical support on the battlefield though was still inadequate. At Waterloo, for instance, there were fewer than 25 doctors and no 'flying ambulances' as had been employed for the French army. Of the 21,000 British soldiers, 1,759 were killed and over 6,000 wounded. It took days to evacuate the wounded from the battlefield who, according to a contemporary account, remained 'in hundreds without any covering, lying on every spare piece of ground. These the medical men were attending. The medical officers were quite worn out with the incessant duty they had been called upon to perform for three successive nights, and still there appeared no end to their toil'.

The battlefield injuries were largely due to musket shot and cannon balls, but also from lance, sabre and bayonet. The most common treatments were bloodletting and amputation, and even if the soldier survived the day, many died of the dreaded consequences of sepsis, suppuration and gangrene. Wounds to the head or abdomen were the most feared, and once the peritoneum or dura was breached death was almost inevitable. Pain relief was mainly with alcohol, and the annals of Waterloo are full of tales of bravery. When the right arm of the future Lord Raglan (of Crimea fame) was amputated he uttered not 'a groan or a sigh' but announced 'Hallo, don't carry that arm away till I have taken off the ring!"

PHYSICIANS IN THE WARS AGAINST THE FRENCH

From the point of view of the Royal College of Physicians, the first to consider is Sir Lucas Pepys (1742–1830; PRCP 1804–11), although he certainly did not endow the College reputation with any reflected glory. Educated at Eton and Christ Church, Oxford, and the son of a banker, Sir Lucas was obvious College material. He had a large practice, enhanced no doubt by his appointment as physician-extraordinary – and then in 1792 as physician-in-ordinary – to the King. He was first Censor, then Treasurer and then President of the College, and in this was damned with faint praise by medical historian William Munk as punctual and assiduous, and a person of 'great firmness and determination, somewhat dictatorial in his bearing, and formed to command'. Academically he seems weak, with his only published work being a Latin preface to the *London Pharmacopœia* of 1809. He gained some historical notoriety in retrospect as opining to the committee of the House of Commons, convened in January 1789 to discuss the health of George III, that the King was showing signs of improvement and would recover in time. This was one of many errors. His prominence and perhaps his commanding personality resulted in his appointment in 1794 as physician-general to the army, on the death of the excellent Sir Clifton Wintringham (1710–94; FRCP 1763) whose monument in Westminster Abbey declares '*ui domi, militiæque, tam in re medicâ insignis, quam ob vitæ innocentiam morumque suavitatem percharus, fiebilis omnibus*'. Pepys was in the same year appointed President of the Army Medical Board and this proved a disastrous step.

> His incompetence in this post was matched only by his arrogance. Pepys had no experience of army medicine and no intention of gaining any.

His contributions to military medicine were, in summary, almost wholly detrimental. As President of the Army Medical Board, he was in charge of all the army's medical arrangements for fifteen years. His incompetence in this post was matched only by his arrogance. Pepys had no experience of army medicine and no intention of gaining any. It was in his gift to appoint all the army physicians and he arbitrarily decided to restrict their numbers drastically, appointing only fourteen physicians in fifteen years. He refused to consider anyone who was not a licentiate or fellow of the College and who was not a graduate of Oxford or Cambridge; as a result none of his appointees had any military experience, nor had been engaged in military medicine. This created a storm of criticism, not least from the more able doctors in lower ranks and from the military surgeons. The physicians were criticised as being 'too fine for common use' and able to 'read Hippocrates in original Greek … but never to have touched a bleeding wound'.

His mismanagement of the army medical services came to a head during the Walcheren crisis in 1809. Napoleon's navy near the port of Antwerp was considered to be a 'pistol held at the head of England', and in 1809 the largest British expeditionary force ever

The Grand Expedition or the Commanders in Chief watching each other's motions – Walcheren. George Cruikshank 1809. A carefully chosen title

assembled was sent to the island of Walcheren to engage the enemy. The expedition was a complete disaster, crippled by an epidemic of Walcheren Fever that largely destroyed the army. Although Walcheren Fever was at the time considered a great mystery, it is now thought to have been due to a medley of malaria, typhus, typhoid and dysentery. The condition affected forty per cent of the troops, and sixty officers and 3,900 soldiers died. Even six months later 11,000 men remained registered sick – compare this to the only 106 men killed in fighting there – and many of those who survived the fever were left apparently permanently debilitated. Walcheren Fever should not have been a surprise, for the inhabitants of the Scheldt were notoriously unhealthy and previous armies had suffered high levels of sickness too. The 'weather and the wet surrounds encouraged ill-health … [and its inhabitants are] pale and listless, suffering much from scrofula, the children rickety, and all much deformed' according to a contemporary account. The French soldiers in contrast were said to be 'as active as ever, and as merry as a beggar under a hedge', as the afflicted English 'pined, drooped, and die'. The condition rendered the men 'listless, prone to yawning, suffering from intense thirst, from shivering and burning fits, and finally falling into complete prostration'. Men died hourly at the height of the epidemic and all burials were ordered to be by night without candles or torches or military bands; coffins were said to be littering the dismal landscape. A parliamentary enquiry later investigated this catastrophe. Pepys appeared before the committee but performed dismally. He had declined to go personally to Walcheren and when asked why, explained that he was not acquainted with the diseases of soldiers in camp. He was heavily criticised and it was concluded that due to the inadequacies of the Army Medical Board, there were far too few doctors present with the troops and the organisation for looking after the sick was chaotic and inadequate. There were no medicines or supplies: apparently the one effective herbal, Peruvian bark – popularised by Sir Hans Sloane (1660–1753; PRCP 1719–35; FRS) – had to be commandeered from an American ship in the vicinity by chance. Parliament was highly critical of the Board and it was thenceforth disbanded. Pepys was humiliated but Dr Munk remarked that after years of ineptitude, he still received a liberal pension for life.

One long-running battle Pepys did have to engage with was with a fellow physician, Robert Jackson (1750–1827; LRCP), now considered one of the great medical doctors of the Napoleonic War. He was a classical scholar who had written extensively on military medicine in the West Indies and served in the American War of Independence. In 1793, he entered the military medical service as a surgeon and desired to be elevated to the post of physician, but Pepys' new rules about being educated at Oxford or Cambridge and a licentiate or fellow of the College excluded him. He appealed, pointing out his scholarship in the area, and Pepys replied: 'Had you the knowledge of Sydenham or of Radcliffe, you are the surgeon of a regiment, and the surgeon of a regiment can never be allowed to be a physician to His Majesty's army'. There followed a decade of acrimony fuelled by false accusations by Pepys about Jackson's practice, and they remained locked in conflict for many years. Reports, pamphlets and letters were published and at one point Jackson was sentenced to six months in the King's Bench Prison for striking Pepys' colleague, the Surgeon General Thomas Keate, with his cane. However, after Pepys' ignominious removal, Jackson was appointed a physician to the army, became a licentiate of the RCP, and made distinguished contributions to military medicine. It is Jackson, the 'Jack-ass', who is seated on the ass in Rowlandson's famous cartoon (see pages overleaf).

The third important physician of the wars against the French was Sir James McGrigor (1771–1858; FRCP 1825). The contrast between him and Lucas Pepys could not be greater. It is difficult to think of a more important figure in military medicine in

Detail from *The Field of Waterloo*. J.M.W. Turner 1818 (© Tate, London 2016)

the nineteenth century, and Sir James' contributions were extensive and have endured. He joined the army in 1793 and within a year had contracted typhus while encamped in the damp and marshy island of Jersey. He survived to serve in the West Indies and India and in 1811 was appointed surgeon-general to Wellington's army. In this position he at last had the authority to begin to make the major changes to the Army Medical Services for which he was so justly praised. He was knighted in 1814 and five days before the Battle of Waterloo in 1815 he was appointed Director-General of the Army Medical Service. As a result of his service, McGrigor was created a Baronet in 1831 and a KCB in 1850, and also served as physician-extraordinary to King George IV and William IV and then to Queen Victoria, and as Lord Rector of the University of Aberdeen. McGrigor published an autobiography and 'Medical Sketches', both providing vivid descriptions of the brutal diseases and medical care of Wellington's army. In the Peninsular Wars, he was responsible for a network of hospitals and systems of care on the battlefield and in the army encampments, and the arrangements for care of casualties greatly improved, work now considered to have been a vital factor in Wellington's success. He later instituted a system of records of the health of the soldiers, which proved pivotal in the mid-century recommendations for improving the health of the army. The detailed and accurate data from the records led, as *The Lancet* put it, 'to the salvation of thousands of lives'. He was also instrumental in preventing disease by improving accommodation for soldiers, their clothing, their food

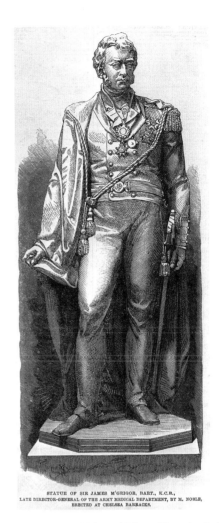

STATUE OF SIR JAMES M'GRIGOR, BART., K.C.B., LATE DIRECTOR-GENERAL OF THE ARMY MEDICAL DEPARTMENT, BY M. NOBLE, ERECTED AT CHELSEA BARRACKS.

Statue of James McGrigor (Wellcome Library, London)

and implementing rigorous medical checks on recruitment, and he too can be credited as being largely responsible for the creation of the Royal Army Medical Corps (RAMC). The reputation of physicians, which had fallen to a new low in Pepys' time, had began to recover. An obelisk to his memory was installed in Aberdeen and a statue in Westminster as a sign of genuine admiration.

THE WINDING UP OF THE MEDICAL REPOR

The Walcheren inquiry into the misconduct of the Army Medical Board of three, resulting in its abolition. Thomas Rowlandson 1810. In the double pillory, signed 'Medical Board', are Lucas Pepys and the Surgeon-General Thomas Keate (with a banner hanging between them proclaiming 'look ass peeps'. Below the pillory is Robert Jackson (A Jacks-son) on a triumphant ass. In the foreground are four soldiers (inscribed 'Sent home for Inspection') dying no doubt of Walcheren Fever, blamed on Pepys. On the left is the Goose Inn, with a sign 'A Goose Cured here'.

PEEPS

OARD

A JACKS -SON

For Home Consumption

For the Hospital

TK TK TK TK TK TK TK TK TK TK TK TK TK TK TK TK

York

Hospital

Clarel

York Hospital

Clarel TK

PORT

N°19

PORT

BUR GUN DY

TK

48th Regiment

TK

Chelsea Hospital

CHAMPAIGN CHEST

London Pub.d March 30.th 1810 by J

HE WALCHEREN EXPEDITION.

Lying around are ineffective remedies marked 'Stores for Walcheren' including a barrel of arsenic for Walcheren, a parcel of oak bark, a container of vitriol, one inscribed 'Powder of Rotten Post' (an allusion to Samuel Butler's satire on medical nonsense), one inscribed 'Cobwebs', and a bottle of gin. Keate is supposed to have siphoned off supplies for his own profits, and on the right are barrels all inscribed TK marked 'For the Hospital' or 'For Home Consumption', and a large 'Champaign Chest', and a turtle inscribed 'TK'. (Wellcome Library, London)

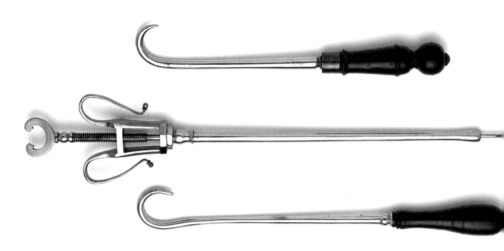

Bullet extractors, Royal College of Physicians museum

MEDICINE IN THE WARS

Casualty figures in the military were large. Between 1793 and 1815, the British army lost 240,000 men. Weaponry had become more sophisticated and lethal, and wounds from bullets and swords in battle caused terrible and disfiguring injury – but in fact, of these deaths only 30,000 or so were due to wounds. The majority were caused by epidemic infectious disease, such as malaria and yellow fever in India and the West Indies, plague and dysentery in Egypt and the Middle East, and typhus, malaria and dysentery in Europe. Ophthalmia was an incurable purulent disease of the eye and alcohol was another potent cause of ill-health, as were syphilis (*le gros lot*) and gonorrhoea (*le petit lot*), both of which spread through the ranks at various times (as was said, 'an hour with Venus and a lifetime with Mercury').

When in Bombay, McGrigor recorded the commonest diseases affecting the regiment as tetanus, cholera, dysentery, hepatitis, pneumonia, measles, scurvy, ophthalmia, venereal disease and Guinea worm. Of course there was also the universal and very annoying 'Malabar itch' (ringworm of the crotch).

In battle, treatments amounted in effect to surgical debridement, dressings and amputation. Musket balls caused grievous injuries, often compound fractures, and the best hope of survival lay in rapid amputation, the surgical wound being less likely to result in gangrene or tetanus than the bullet. Operations were usually carried out in a makeshift theatre with, for instance, a farmhouse door as the table. There was no anaesthetic, except the pint of rum. Amputations were often performed

OPPOSITE: Detail from *The meeting of Wellington and Blücher after Waterloo.* Daniel Maclise 1858 (© Royal Academy of Arts, London; Photographer: Prudence Cuming Associates Ltd)

with blunt instruments and the injured soldiers were evacuated from the battlefield to a dressing station and then, usually by peasants' wagon carts, to regimental hospitals. The conditions were appalling and many died in hospital, the great majority from dysentery, fever, gangrene or typhus. The bravery of the soldiers undergoing amputations in these horrifying settings is astounding and there are many stories of extraordinary fortitude.

The role of the physician in battle, in contrast to the surgeon, was to stand on the sidelines and to deal with the derelict residuum after the day was done. In comparison with the effectiveness of surgery, the medical treatment given out to the military was farcical. The contents of one typical regimental medical chest, for instance, comprised forty-four medicines, ranging from ammonia to sulphuric acid, gum Arabic to senna, Spanish soap and wine to mercury and rhubarb, ginger and verdigris. How much harm was done by such treatments is not recorded.

'Antiphlogistic' treatment was usually given to infections, comprising purging and emetics, cold water, warm baths and blood-letting, and lots of opium for dysentery. Cold water treatment for malaria was another popular remedy. Assistant surgeon Walter Henry described his own 'water' treatment for malaria:

[His doctor] sheared and shaved my curly locks one hot afternoon, and attached three dozen of leeches to my poor caput. A few hours after, they carried me into the yard, placed me erect, and poured four or five-and-twenty buckets of cold well-water over me from a third floor window, after this terrible shower-bath, I was rubbed dry and put to bed. For the first two hours I was not quite sure whether my head had not been carried away in the flood, for I felt as if there was no living part, and all was numb and cold above my shoulders but there was a violent reaction during the night and I became delirious the next morning.

Still, he survived!

For the physicians, though, all was not bad. James McGrigor, with the Indian Army in Egypt in 1801, describes his tented accommodation:

I had upwards of a dozen Indian servants, with their wives, besides my English soldier servant, and for my stock three camels, two horses, twenty-four sheep, three goats, several dozen of fowls, with a good many pigeons, rabbits, etc. My own large Indian marquee was in the centre, and around were the small Arab tents which my Indian servants had raised for themselves. In another quarter were my animals and a store tent ... I can never forget the astonishment of some officers of the English army ... they told me that I brought to their mind the age of patriarchs of old, with their herds, their flocks, their man-servants and their maid-servants.

In the Peninsular Wars though, sadly his accommodation was much more spartan.

At sea, too, physicians made their contribution. Sir Gilbert Blane (1747–1834; LRCP 1781; FRS) was physician to the West Indies Fleet and a Commissioner of Sick and Hurt, and was most celebrated in these positions for his advocacy of lemon juice as a compulsory ration for all sailors, thus preventing scurvy, the deficiency of vitamin C, which had hitherto been the major cause of disease in the British Navy. Indeed, scurvy was said to have killed more sailors than enemy action, with estimates that two million sailors between 1500 and 1800 died from the deficiency. John Shipp, a (well-named) lieutenant in the eighty-seventh regiment, gives a graphic description of his experiences of scurvy:

My poor legs were as big as drums, and my gums swollen to an enormous size, and my tongue too big for my mouth. All I could eat was raw potatoes and vinegar ... We were all so reduced by suffering that even strong men could not restrain themselves from weeping, they knew not why. And so the time went by, men dying in dozens, and almost before the breath was out of their bodies being thrown into the sea for the sharks to quarrel over.

Blane did not discover the protective effect of lemon juice, which was conclusively shown by the investigations of James Lind (a member of the Edinburgh not the London College), but he was one of the small band of physicians who were instrumental in introducing lemons into the naval diet. At the time, the commonly accepted theory, proposed by the Surgeon-General and President of the Royal Society Sir John Pringle (1707–82; FRCP 1763; FRS), among others, was that scurvy was due to a lack of 'fixed air' in body tissue, which could be prevented by drinking infusions of malt and wort whose fermentation in the body would replace the missing air. Blane flew in the face of this medical orthodoxy and based his recommendations on carefully collected statistics, which were a hallmark of his work. Blane also wrote the influential report on the mortality rates during the fiasco at Walcheren, which resulted in the withdrawal of the troops from the island, as well as reports on quarantine, military and civilian hygiene, keeping infectious diseases out of prisons and hulks, and the transportation of convicts. He was notoriously cold in temperament, steely under fire in the Navy, and in civilian life sometimes known as 'Chillblanc'. His focus throughout his life though was firmly on the prevention of disease, and by 1813, Blane could claim from the study of mortality figures that improvements in medical care in the Navy since 1779 were such that over 6,000 fewer lives were being lost per year.

The nineteenth century, after the fall of Napoleon, provided no respite for Britain and its armed forces. As the British Empire expanded Colonial wars took place in every decade – Maratha wars, Xhosa wars, Afghanistan, Burma, the 'Indian Mutiny', and many others. Two remain still vivid in the present day – the Crimean War and the Boer War.

Florence Nightingale in the Military Hospital at Scutari. James Bentwell (Wellcome Library, London)

THE CRIMEA WAR: FLORENCE NIGHTINGALE AND THE COLLEGE OF PHYSICIANS

The war in the Crimea, 1853–56, ranged Britain, France, the decaying Ottoman Empire and Sardinia against Russia. Its origins were confused in the complex politics of the period, but in popular memory two images survive – the Charge of the Light Brigade and Florence Nightingale, 'the lady with the lamp'.

I won't have the College of physicians represented, nor the apothecaries. What! Give the franchise to the greatest credulity in the world, to the blindest adherence to prejudice and procrastination – to the most obstinate opposition to all fact and experience – don't give it to the physicians or I'll get up an examination and everyone of them will be plucked. You may give it to the surgeons if you like because they are better.

This view certainly exemplifies Florence Nightingale's relationship with doctors in a confrontation that came to a head when she arrived in Turkey, and persisted for many years after. 'That old smoke-dried' Sir Andrew Smith (1797–1872; FRCP 1860), Inspector-General and Superintendent of the Army Medical Department, was one

The Valley of the Shadow of Death (Sevastapol road after the battle). Roger Fenton 1855 (Digital image courtesy of the Getty's Open Content Program)

of her antagonists, held up as a die-hard enemy of reform. He was heavily censured by the press for mismanagement after *The Times'* correspondents' notorious reports on the state of the hospital at Scutari after the battle of Alma: 'it is with feelings of surprise and anger that the public will learn that no sufficient preparation has been made for the care of the wounded … not sufficient surgeons … no dressers and nurses … nor even linen to bandage'. The post-war Royal Commission of enquiry took a more measured view of Smith, after he answered the 623 questions put to him in oral session (Florence Nightingale did well when she answered at the enquiry, but then she had written the questions).

Another doctor with whom she fell out in Turkey was John Meyer (1814–70; FRCP 1863). He had accompanied a band of nurses to the Crimea to reinforce Miss Nightingale's efforts, but she took offence as she had not requested this support and most importantly the nurses were not put under her direction. Meyer became superintendent of the British Military Hospital set up at Smyrna, an institution notable for the fact that among the staff recruited were three future Presidents of the Royal College of Surgeons, five professors of medicine at British universities, and four fellows of the Royal Society.

One fellow to whom Miss Nightingale did relate well was Graham Balfour (1813–91; FRCP 1860; FRS). He enlisted in the army two years after qualifying and devoted his career to developing the application of statistical methods. After the official Crimean Enquiry his studies laid down the future pattern of health returns of the

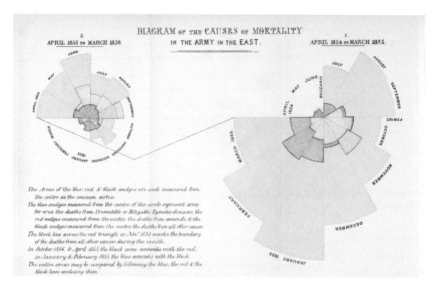

Causes of death in the Crimean War month by month 1854–56. Florence Nightingale. Infection vastly outnumbers all others (Wellcome Library, London)

British Army. It was Florence Nightingale who 'arranged' for his membership of the Enquiry panel – reflecting no doubt her own interest in mathematics and statistical methods, exemplified by her mapping of causes and site of death during the Crimean campaign. Those illustrated in blue were 'preventable or mitigatable Zymotic diseases'; this work was immensely influential in the future planning of army medical services.

THE BOER WAR

During the last years of the nineteenth century festering resentment between descendants of the former Dutch colonists of South Africa and the South African – British colonial – government culminated in a three-year war. It was the first of three wars in which Colonel Philip Stock (1876–1975; FRCP 1937) served. He enlisted in the RAMC and joined the 8th Hussars as regimental medical officer. His photographic and written records illustrate the minimal nature of the equipment available in South Africa and document the ground plans of a number of military hospitals and designs for sanitary stations. Later, during World War I, he organised the medical services for the invasion of German South-West Africa – now Namibia – including suborning General Botha, the general commanding the invasion, to undergo public anti-typhoid vaccination on the parade ground. During World War II, in charge of health in London air-raid shelters, Stock and his colleagues tracked down and identified the obscure mosquito *Culex pipiens molestus*, long-breeding in waste water in the London Underground and invigorated by the night-time use of stations as shelters.

ABOVE: *Mules hauling the Medical Equipment of the 8th Hussars during the Boer War.* Photo Col Philip Stock
PAGES OVERLEAF: *Plan of Boer War Military Hospital for 20 Officers and 500 men – demonstrating sites of tents, latrines, water filters etc.* Col Philip Stock (All photography Mike Fear)

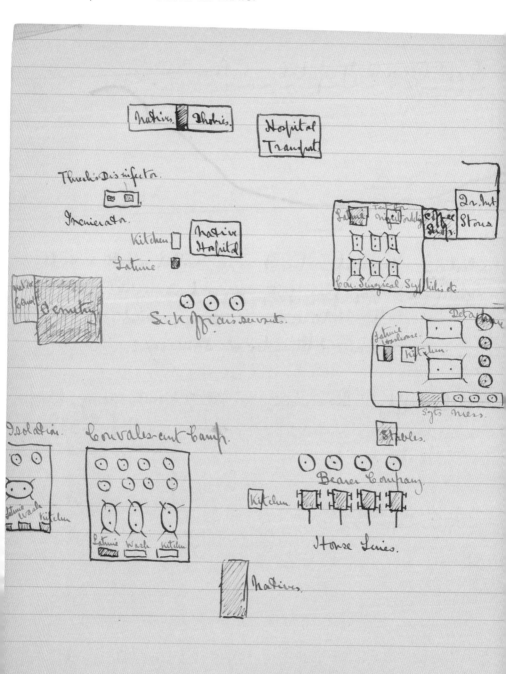

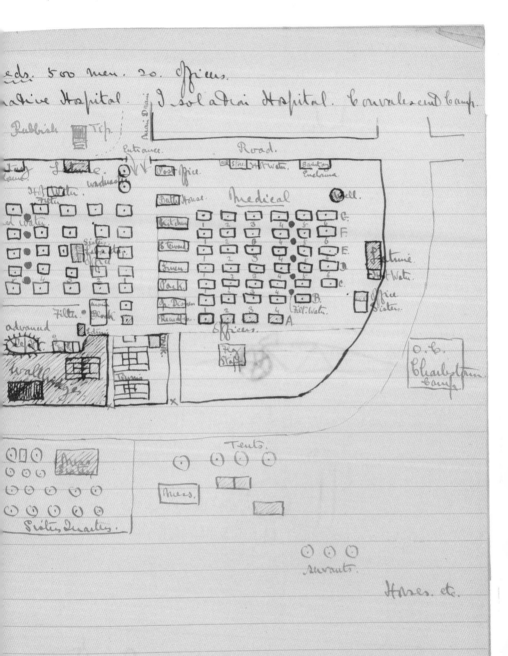

WORLD WAR I

On 4 August 1914, war was declared on Germany, but Britain and its medical services were ill-prepared for the level of military casualties. Of the 8.9 million men enlisted from Britain and its Empire over the next four years, around one million were killed and two million wounded. The bloody battles of the Somme claimed 95,000 British and Empire lives and more than 300,000 men were injured. Perhaps for the first time, in this war physicians made significant inroads into disease, and this despite wholly chaotic and adverse conditions.

Wars challenge medicine, but at the same time stimulate novel medical thinking and therapies: hitherto unexplained diseases assume epidemic proportions and ailments both minor and major appear in new light. In World War I, four 'new' phenomena became of particular medical importance: trench fever, shell shock, gas warfare and missile injury to the head. These conditions challenged the ingenuity of British medicine and many fellows of the College became deeply involved in defining their clinical presentations and devising new treatments.

THE COLLEGE AND WORLD WAR I

As an institution the College had a quiet war. The minutes of the 24 September 1914 College meeting, the first after the outbreak of hostilities, show little evidence that the most destructive war in human history had commenced. A meeting of the Royal College of Surgeons was reported, a future international conference was discussed, and a fellow requested permission to reproduce a portrait of Dr John Arbuthnot for an encyclopaedia. It was, however, decided not to hold the Harveian Dinner that year.

The Committee of the Joint RCP and Royal College of Surgeons (Conjoint) Examination Board appeared more prescient, recommending on 14 August that up to six months' service in a naval or military hospital could be counted towards qualification as licentiate of the Physicians' college and member of the Surgeons' college.

By October 1914 the Registrar had written to the Secretary of the Admiralty enquiring as to methods of protecting the College from aerial bombardment and had been reassured (perhaps) by the Lords Commissioners of the Admiralty that 'only indiscriminate bomb dropping is to be expected'. Protection of individual buildings was therefore, their lordships concluded, unnecessary as the individual chances of damage were slight. Presumably the anxiety of the College, as well as the logic of the Admiralty's reply, reflected the proximity of the College in Pall Mall to the Admiralty in the Mall. The College's own opinion was that sandbags on the roof would be of little use, and some of the College's most valuable books were moved to the basement strong-room.

Tending the wounded at 'The Shambles' Dunkirk. C.R.W. Nevinson 1916 (© Imperial War Museum (ART 725))

German Zeppelin (© Imperial War Museum (Q 58481))

On 8 September 1915, the first and most devastating Zeppelin air attack of the War on London took place; the famous L13 airship meandered across central London dropping its fifteen high-explosive and fifty-five incendiary bombs. One of these landed fifteen yards away from the College's Examination Hall in Queen Square. Fortunately the only inhabitants at the time – the four children of the caretaker – were asleep in the basement, but almost every window facing the square was broken, window frames blown out and the entrance door blown open. Dramatic and historic though this was, the cost of the damage amounted to only £685 (all recovered from insurance) and the examination scheduled for the following day was transferred to 'another room at the back of the building'. Simultaneous damage in the National Hospital for Nervous Disease on the other side of the square was said to have proved an effective cure for patients with hysterical paralysis, who jumped from their beds and ran for cover. Spurred into action by the event, the College insured its building and contents for £40,000.

In 1915 the Censor's board considered a letter from a fellow proposing the Government should be advised to introduce compulsory inoculation against enteric fever – but no resolution was arrived at. The President did later raise the matter with Sir Alfred Keogh (1857–1936; FRCP 1914), Director-General of the RAMC, who thought it would be 'wise to wait for the moment'.

The College considered a request from the Dean of St Bartholomew's Hospital and from the War Office that regulations be altered to shorten the duration of training for medical students, as additional medical officers were urgently required. The

ON THE NIGHT OF THE EIGHTH OF SEPTEMBER 1915 A ZEPPELIN BOMB FELL AND EXPLODED ON THIS SPOT ALTHOUGH NEARLY ONE THOUSAND PEOPLE SLEPT IN THE SURROUNDING BUILDINGS NO PERSON WAS INJURED

ABOVE: Plaque in Queen Square, London, commemorating Zeppelin raid on 8 September 1915 (www. LondonRemembers.com)
PAGES OVERLEAF: Royal Army Medical Corps in the trenches (Image courtesy of Army Medical Services Museum)

Committee of Management offered a compromise by which education in science prior to entry into medical school could be recognised.

The Government had established its own Central Medical War Committee to 'organise the medical profession in England, Wales and Ireland'. In March 1915, the British Medical Association set up a War Emergency Committee, on which the President of the College was invited to sit – its principal activity seems to have been to safeguard the personal interest and practice of civilian practitioners who volunteered for army work.

The College discussions as to the latter Committee reflect more on the nature of committees than on any urgency. Members sought information about the Committee's standing vis-á-vis the Army Medical Service. The registrar thought fellows should not be co-opted but instead elected to such a committee. The Senior Censor wished only to send a sympathetic message, and the second Censor thought the whole discussion was irregular because no notice of the discussion had been given. The Treasurer commented that the current meeting was a small one and ought not to commit the College. However, eventually the President and the Censors were empowered to take whatever steps they thought advisable. A committee, known initially as the 'Central War Committee' and then as the 'Committee of Reference', was eventually established with the Royal College of Surgeons, chaired by Sir Frederick Taylor (1847–1920; PRCP 1915–18).

It was only in 1916 that the College became seriously engaged with the war effort. In July the College was asked to help in the matter of an acute shortage of medical officers, attributed to the campaign in the Dardanelles. It was already clear that there was a dearth of doctors not only for the army but also at home in the civilian hospitals. In December 1916 the Committee of Reference recommended that all doctors should be mobilised to give service as required by the country. The Comitia initially turned down the resolution, against the advice of the President, but when the Government announced the possibility of compulsory national mobilisation, the College had to modify its stance, asking only that it be in charge of the arrangements being made for doctors. The Committee of Reference obtained the right to refuse enlistment to the military of doctors whose presence was essential to the civilian population – against a background of a grossly unequal distribution of doctors in England from an extreme of one per 850 of the population in London to one in 11,000 in various northern areas. Lists of doctors essential to the functioning of civil hospitals were drawn up. In other recommendations, the Committee suggested to the Government that to minimise interfering with the duties of students who were busy as unqualified House Surgeons, all systematic lectures to them should be discontinued.

Later, the remit of the Committee of Reference was extended from identifying and exempting specific individuals from military service to advising the Government on the care of disabled and wounded soldiers. They argued that discharging such men from the services would deprive them of necessary medical care and prospects for rehabilitation: ninety per cent of such men would be 'of the class coming under the National Health Insurance Commission – i.e. they will be treated by panel doctors': how would these men, imperfectly cured, obtain consultation with and treatment by specialists?

'The strange lady in whose company he was said to have left' was his sister

The College had other bread-and-butter concerns vying for its attention. Dr Kramer, a licentiate of the College, had been accused of having systematically canvassed for patients. He argued that the basis of the accusation came from a claim that he was German – whereas he was in fact Russian – and that the 'the strange lady in whose company he was said to have left' was his sister. A letter was received from the General Medical Council concerning a medical student erased from the Medical Students Register for having obtained money by false pretences – by impersonating a captain in the Royal Army Medical Corps and passing recruits as fit for service. The Censor's board withdrew the licence of a doctor for selling 'at exorbitant prices … and frequent intervals … and otherwise than as a medicine … large quantities of an intoxicant drug named heroin … for an Officer and men, members of His Majesty's forces'. And in April 1917 Dr Taylor expressed surprise that the College had not purchased Consols, considering their low price; the Treasurer replied that as a patriotic institution the College had put all its available cash into War Loans.

By 1918 mention of the war was remarkably sparse in the College annals. More attention was being paid to two areas which had major influences on immediate post-war Britain and indeed resonate to this day. The first was the rising influenza epidemic, magnified in large military hospitals such as Étaples. The College's treatise on the transmission and treatment of influenza is an interesting document 'whilst the nature of the virus is uncertain'. How far the College's advice that 'at the first feeling of illness or rise in temperature the patient should go to bed at once and summon his medical attendant' would be appreciated today is debatable. A second was whether or not the College should get involved in discussions concerning a possible Ministry of Health – the first stirrings of state involvement in the business of medicine.

THE QUATERCENTENARY CELEBRATIONS

The 400th anniversary of the founding of the College was a muted affair. The President, Norman Moore (1847–1922; PRCP 1918–22), reported that:

> . . . when we reflected in what a war we were engaged, more or less every one of us, in defence of our liberties and those of Europe, and indeed all mankind, we felt that we could not at present take part in the happy kind of ceremonial suitable to times of peace.

The President also referred to the fact that although the number of fellows had increased from six to upwards of 300 over the four centuries, no change had taken place in its organisation – an accolade one might hope not to award on the occasion of the 500th anniversary.

However, sixteen fellows of the College, on active service in France, had other ideas and did celebrate the anniversary in Boulogne with a seven-course dinner and fine wines. The fellows produced (with remarkable ingenuity in the fog of war!) and presented the College with an illuminated Latin address on vellum, reflecting not only on the past glories and present intellectual power of the College, but also on the Pandora's box of new diseases. In translation the address reads:

> We, the undersigned members, gathered under arms at Boulogne, send heartiest greetings and congratulations to the Royal College of Physicians of London as it celebrates the fourth centenary of its foundation and embarks upon its fifth. It would be a major task to honour and enumerate so many within our membership who, ceaselessly, have upheld the honour of our College; who have advanced the art of medicine by their learning, and even taught us to restore the bodies of men crushed by disease to full-bodied health. And how rarely does one find a College whose alumni bedeck their learning with both

Menu of the Dinner held in Boulogne to mark
the 400th anniversary of the College
(All photography Mike Fear)

Collegio *Regali Medicorum Londinensium* *quartum saeculum vitae suae feliciter conditum celebranti et quintum jam faustis auspiciis ineunti salutem plurimam dicunt et libentissime gratulantur Socii subsignati, Gesoriaci Bononiensium inter arma collocati. Longum est nomina percurrere tot virorum illustrium qui sine ulla intercapedine continenter honorem Collegii nostri sustulerunt, scientia artem medicinae altius provexerunt, feliciter hominum corpora morbis oppressa ad integram valetudinem revocare docuerunt. Sed quotam quidque invenimus Collegium cujus alumni literas quoque humaniores urbanitate tanta et lepore ornaverint, scientiam omnis generis tutius ingenio aedificaverint, rei publicae insignius profuerint?*

Quarto jam anno belli consensu omnium furore teutonice incepti peracto, militantes videmus eheu! qualis noxa febrium terris incubuerit cohors, velut e Pandorae pyxide liberata, quot morbos pediculi nicnon muscae, quot vapores noxii attulerint, quanta denique strage nostrorum et totius gentis humanae hostis barbarus Marte illacrimabili maxime abusus sit debellandus. Sed sortes jamdudum faustae, florent arma ampliusque florebunt, praevalebit tandem justitia. Quin etiam (cum licet denique) Pheidippidis verbis sine superbia usi, spe victoriae certa Collegium nostrum valedicentes jubemus Χαίρετε, νικῶμεν.

Gesoriaci Bononiensium. A.D.IX *Kal. Oct.* MDCDXVIII

elegance and wit, who have ably built upon knowledge of every kind, who have been of such outstanding benefit to their country. And now in the fourth year of this war, when all agree that the frenzied German attack has been pierced and halted, in our military duties we see, alas, that a vast cohort of new diseases oppresses the earth, as if from Pandora's box. How many disease have lice, flies and poisonous gas brought us. And what carnage of our troops and of the whole human race has been required to vanquish the barbarian host, the enemy who has put ruthless war to its foulest forms. But omens are propitious – our side flourished and will flourish further, and in the end justice will prevail. Indeed it is now possible, in the certain hope of victory, to without boasting employ the words of Pheidippes – 'Be of good cheer – victory is ours'.

Boulogne 23 September 1918

The Germans it seems, thought otherwise, and the dinner was, according to College history, curtailed by enemy action.

FELLOWS IN WAR

Many fellows of the College were sent as young men to the front. Sir John Josias Conybeare (1888–1967; FRCP 1926) was nearly qualified when war broke out and immediately left for active service in the Oxfordshire and Buckingham Light Infantry. His 1915 diary records life in and behind the trenches with what nowadays appears a surprisingly light touch:

April 1915

It is a great thing to have a bed for the night, even if it being shared with two others ...

I am just beginning to suffer from lack of tobacco. I wish the British American Tobacco Company would hurry up and send my parcel along.

[From the Argyll and Sutherland Highland trenches] The Germans are rather further off, about 250 yards in most places. They are either Saxons or Bavarians and seem quite friendly.

On the whole, life in the trenches is pleasant enough. It would be much more so were it not for the interference of the Brigade and Regimental Staff, who are all the most cowardly, chicken hearted set of meddling fools ever born.

Moved to the Piggeries about one mile from here ... The men are all in pigsties, which make very comfortable beds for four men apiece.

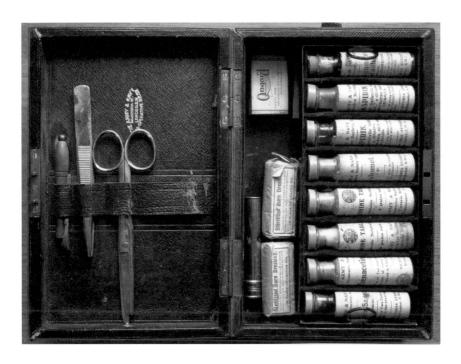

Medical kit from the Army & Navy Stores – note very basic contents: aspirin, phenacetin, quinine, calomel
(Courtesy of Dr Andrew Bamjii)

June 1915

Another lot of anti-gas appliances issued. Each man now has a smoke
helmet with mica eyepiece, and also as a reserve a respirator. All our old
respirators have been withdrawn and burnt. This is now the fourth issue of
respirators we have had and I don't know how many memos have come
round 'cancelling all previous instructions' ... Went into the Chateau grounds
... some splendid strawberries but they are not ripe ... the Chateau is said
to belong to Hennessey, the brandy man. It must have been a most beautiful
place, but now after nearly six months of almost daily bombardment it is
little more than a ruin.

He won the Military Cross on the Somme and returned to England in 1916 when the
army recalled all senior medical students serving as combatants. After qualification
he returned to the war in Mesopotamia. In peace he became physician at Guy's and
author of a famous textbook.

Others stayed at home. Lord Russell Brain (1895–1966; PRCP 1950–57) was an
Oxford undergraduate reading history in 1914. He joined the Friends' Ambulance

ABOVE: *A lecture on gas protection.* Horace Bury 1916 (Wellcome Library, London)
PAGES OVERLEAF: *The Wounded at Dover.* Sir John Lavery 1918 (© Imperial War Museum (ART 1273))

Brigade as a conscientious objector and was sent to the Haxby Hospital near York, set up in the Dining Block of Rowntree's Chocolate Factory. His diary recounts his innovative work as a radiological technician, with reflections on militarism and a record of daily life. After the war he went back to Oxford to read medicine.

> *... we had one case to X-ray of a man with a bullet in his chest. We made two exposures on the same plate, moving the table between, in order to localize the bullet – the precise method would take too long to explain – and as there was no variation of the image on the plate the bullet should be just under the skin. Which it is not. The little puzzle awaits solution ... I also set up two stereoscopic photos of a rifle bullet in a man's knee. We have two illuminated screens side by side on which we place two photos taken from slightly different positions, and the pictures are reflected by two mirrors in the centre, to the eyes ...*

I never realized quite so vividly before how truly this is an old man's war. It is the old men who made the war, and it is the old men who bleat for blood. But the young men, though they say very little about it, and accept the hell that is made for them, know deep in their hearts the folly and futility of the whole thing. I have little fear of militarism after the war, for the men who have been into battle will never believe a militarist again ... [how wrong he turned out to be] ... a convoy ... arrived between nine and ten this morning ... of 80 men. They came with all the grime of French soil on their uniforms, and all the weariness of war in their eyes. One, I noticed, had wire cutters hanging from his belt. Most of them limped, some could hardly walk. Their bandages were rough and ready. No fewer than 20 were cases of gas poisoning from our own gas, caused partly by a change in the wind which blew our gas back in our own trenches, partly by the explosion of a German shell among our gas cylinders. Of the 33 of these which have lately come from the front, no fewer than 9 were cases of injuries to the fingers or hand, and of the rest 11 were cases of gunshot wound in the elbow. This is an extraordinary proportion. The number of finger cases is explained, by those who know, as being due to self inflicted injury. The elbow injuries, most of which are on the left side are due to the position of the left arm and elbow when firing over the edge of the trench ...

I never realized quite so vividly before how truly this is an old man's war. It is the old men who made the war, and it is the old men who bleat for blood.

Dr. Muir is interested in the case of the man M— with the bullet in his back and saw the plate directly it was finished. He told me to X-ray the man again for localization. This I did, localizing it both from in front and behind, and taking two stereoscopic photos. I also marked it in the skin of his back. I was able, therefore, to send in this report. 'Double exposures made for localization from anterior and posterior aspects show round shrapnel bullet 1 inch to right of 4th lumbar vertebra at depth of 1 ¼ inches from posterior aspect.' Dr. B— came up this evening and made an entirely different report on the strength of his simple photo. Dr. Muir and Dr. Lang came down this evening to look at my plates and I succeeded in convincing them that I was right and Dr. B. wrong and the man was brought in and I did him again in their presence and pointed out the bullet immediately under my mark ...

At 8.15 I took the chair at a meeting of the Debating Society. The motion 'that this house believes in fairies' was carried by 12 votes to 11.

... So ended a very busy day.

Sir Wilmot Herringham (Taken from *A physician in France*, 1919)

The first consultant physician to the army was Sir Wilmot Herringham (1855–1936; FRCP 1889), physician at St Bartholomew's Hospital and commanding officer of the medical unit of London Universities Officer Training corps in 1914. He was rapidly seconded to the First London General Hospital set up in a board school in Camberwell, staffed exclusively by doctors and nurses from Barts. He was at the time University Vice Chancellor and needed the permission of the University Senate when he took the role of consulting physician to the army in October. He was the first such, but by the end of the war each of the five British armies in France had its own consulting physician. In 1916 he was appointed to the Committee on Treatment of Gas Diseases, together with Sir Almroth Wright (1861–1947; FRCP 1938), T.R. Elliott (1877–1961; FRCP 1915) and C.G. Douglas. At the end of the war he published a memoir *A Physician in France*: an idiosyncratic and wide-ranging book, commencing with reflections on the differences between the English and German character. He describes the organisation of the RAMC; the distribution of advanced dressing stations, clearing stations and base hospitals; the issues that arose in respect of the status of medical officers; the unfairness that doctors who had enrolled as territorials before the war maintained the rank they had reached, while those seconded during the war were appointed at a higher rank; the state of English dentistry – 'the English need to encourage dentistry, for the simple reason that they are so disgustingly dirty'; and opines on military matters and war poetry ('poor'). He pays huge tribute to

C.R.W. NEVINSON.

:ht Arrival of Wounded.

Night Arrival of Wounded. C.R.W. Nevinson 1915 (Image courtesy of Army Medical Services Museum)

the pathology service and the elucidation of conditions such as cerebrospinal fever (meningococcal as it transpired) and its unpredictable epidemiology. He describes the experiments performed to identify the aetiology of the novel relapsing condition Trench Fever – including the importation and quarantine of lice from England for experimental inoculations, to bite sufferers and then attempt to infect others.

Other reflections are on the French way of life, their art of conversation and how they bring up children. And in a section on hospitals – he spent some weeks with back problems – he sums up the dress of English nurses as ugly.

> *I also wish that English girls would not wear their skirts quite so short. The English leg is I am sorry to say highly inelegant, whereas the French are very neat, and when you get a really good view of the whole leg up to just below the knee the contrast is distressing.*

After the war he declined an invitation to succeed Sir William Osler as Regius Professor of Medicine in Oxford. He also edited and wrote large parts of the *Official History of the Great War* related to medical services, an enormous and comprehensive work of reference and a triumph of scholarship.

ABOVE: *Our men on leave in Paris. A dance at the British Army and Navy Leave Club.* J. Simont 1918 (Wellcome Library, London)
LEFT: *Interior of a Hospital Tent 1918.* John Singer Sargent (© Imperial War Museum (ART 1611))

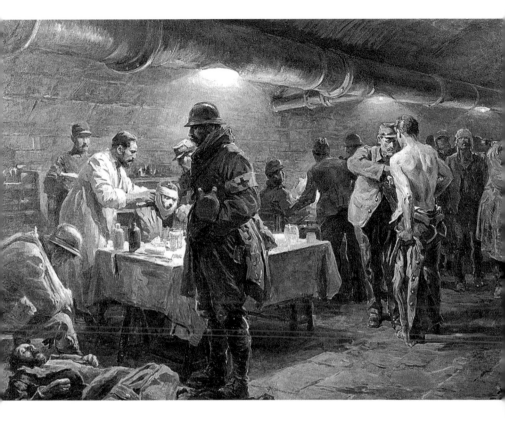

ABOVE: *Advanced Dressing Station 1917*. Artist unknown (Wellcome Library, London) LEFT: Foot Inspection, 12th battalion East Yorkshire Regiment (© Imperial War Museum (Q 10622))

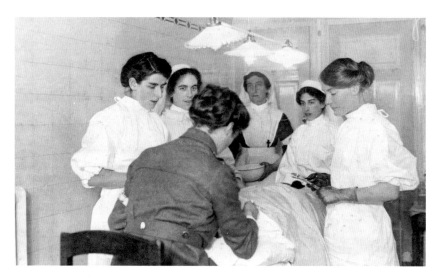

Members of the Women's Hospital Corps operating in Paris 1914 in the Hotel Astoria (or Hotel Claridge). The chloroform is being administered by the Surgeon-in-Charge Dr Flora Murray (seated, seen from the back) assisted by Dr Majorie Blandy (right). (© Imperial War Museum (HU 90880))

WOMEN DOCTORS

Women were determined to play their part. Dr Louisa Garrett Anderson was a supporter of Mrs Pankhurst's Women's Social and Political Union and a radical activist. She had been imprisoned for a month with hard labour in Holloway Prison in 1912 for throwing a brick and breaking a window following a speech by an anti-suffragist Cabinet minister. At the onset of war in 1914 she strode into the French Embassy in London, offering to raise money for and to equip a surgical unit of women doctors and nurses for service in France. Within weeks, on 17 September 1914, Louisa Garrett Anderson was in Paris: 'We found Claridge's Hotel a gorgeous shell of marble and gilt without heating or crockery or anything practical but by dint of mild "militancy" and unending push things have advanced immensely.' She set up her hospital there with her colleagues Drs Flora Murray and Gertrude Gazdar.

> *The cases that come to us are very septic and the wounds are terrible ...*
> *We have fitted up quite a satisfactory small operating theatre in the 'Ladies*
> *Lavatory' which has tiled floor and walls, good water supply & heating. I*
> *bought a simple operating table in Paris and we have arranged gas ring and*
> *fish kettles for sterilization ... after years of unpopularity over the suffrage*
> *it is very exhilarating to be on top of the wave, helped and approved by*
> *everyone, except perhaps the English War Office, while all the time we are*
> *doing suffrage work ... I wish the whole organization for the care of the*

wounded … could be put into the hands of women. This is not military work. It is merely a matter of organisation, common sense, attention to detail and a determination to avoid unnecessary suffering and loss of life.

Other women's hospitals were also opened in France, including the hospital in the Abbaye de Royaumont, run by the Scottish Women's Hospitals. This had 600 beds and was the largest voluntary hospital in France, where the remarkable Dr Frances Ivens, later to be the first female consultant in Liverpool, was in charge. On 25 September 1915 Miss M. Starr, a VAD (Voluntary Aid Detachment), wrote of a new casualty at Royaumont:

One arm will simply have to be amputated, he had had poison gas, as well, and the smell was enough to knock one down, bits of bone sticking out and all gangrene. It will be marvellous if Miss Ivens saves it, but she is going to try it appears, as it is his right arm. He went to X-ray, then to Theatre, and I believe the operation was rather wonderful, but I had no time to stop and see.

Due to political pressure, not least because of the war service of female doctors, in 1925 the College, which had steadfastly previously refused to allow women to apply for fellowship, changed its bye-laws in 1925 and the first female fellow was eventually elected in 1934.

The Scottish Women's Hospital. In The Cloister of the Abbaye at Royaumont. Dr Frances Ivens inspecting a French patient. Norah Neilson-Gray 1920 (© Imperial War Museum (ART 3090))

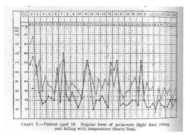

Chart I.—Patient aged 19. Regular form of pulse-rate (light line) rising and falling with temperature (heavy line).

Temperature chart in trench fever (HMSO, London)

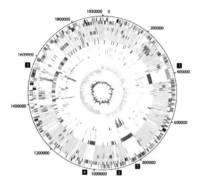

Genome of *Bartonella quintana* (Alsmark CM, Frank AC, Karlberg EO *et al.* The louse-borne human pathogen *Bartonella quintana* is a genomic derivative of the zoonotic agent *Bartonella henselae*. *Proceedings of the National Academy of Sciences of the United States of America* 2004;101:9716–9721, Fig 1. (c) National Academy of Sciences, USA, 2004)

This was indeed a new disease and became seen as a paradigmatic example of how effective medical research carried out in the field could be, despite the disruptions and distractions of battle.

TRENCH FEVER

Herringham played an important role in describing and elucidating the cause of one of the 'new diseases' of World War I – Trench Fever. First recorded among the British troops in Salonika in 1915, and then more widely in the German, French and British armies, the condition was characterised by a five-day relapsing fever with severe headache and pain in the back and the legs, a rash and general malaise. A slightly enlarged spleen was often detected. The medical journals debated whether this really was a new disease, as Herringham had determined. Others held that this simply a variant of other infectious disorders such as enteric fever or typhus, perhaps modified by inoculation. The condition was not fatal but did require bed rest and convalescence and was a cause of considerable wastage in the theatre of war. It has been estimated that about one million soldiers were infected, including 380,000 in the British Expeditionary Force, and such was the perceived threat to the war effort that the War Office established a Trench Fever Investigation Commission to study the disease. Almost immediately, an infective basis transmitted by *Pediculus corporis*, the louse common in the trenches, was proposed, and various organisms including spirochaetes and protozoa transmitted by the louse were purported to be the cause. The Commission carried out meticulous research and the true culprit was identified, a rickettsia body, an organism subsequently named *Rickettsia quintana*. This was indeed a new disease and became seen as a paradigmatic example of how effective medical research carried out in the field could be, despite the disruptions and distractions of battle. After the war the condition virtually disappeared through effective delousing measures applied to returning soldiers, although it resurfaced again in the similar conditions of World War II. In the 1990s, genomic analysis allowed the reclassification of the organism as *Bartonella quintana*.

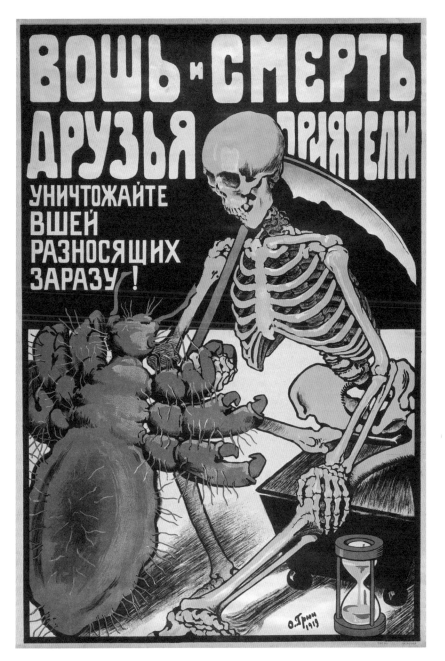

The typhus louse shaking hands with Death. O. Grin 1919 (Wellcome Library, London)

SHELL SHOCK

Cases of shell shock began to appear within a few months of the onset of hostilities on the Western Front and this seemed to be another 'new disease'. The military reaction was universally highly unsympathetic and the soldiers were generally considered 'scrimshankers'. There was a professional debate about whether the condition was a manifestation of psychoneurosis or a physical effect of blast injury (the former explanation gaining ascendency as the war progressed) and British physicians were deeply involved. Initially it was planned to evacuate the cases back to psychiatric hospitals in England, but as the numbers rose this proved impossible and a series of forward treatment centres just behind the lines was created to treat men without evacuation. A variety of treatment approaches were taken, a major aim of which was to get the soldiers back to a state in which they could be returned to the front lines, and it was recognised that the longer the condition persisted the less likely rapid recovery was. Hypnosis, abreaction and other methods of suggestion were used by some physicians to demonstrate the 'false' nature of the neurological symptoms. Others evolved a treatment regimen involving rest, medication to induce sleep and a programme of graduated exercise, with some ending with route marches. Military impatience persisted and in January 1917, the psychologically oriented Charles Myers was relieved of his command and replaced by the neurologist Gordon Morgan Holmes (1876–1965; FRCP 1914; FRS), who had little patience or sympathy with psychological approaches to shell shock and was contemptuous of hysterics. He was concerned that transferring patients out of the military area would lead to a flood of copycat cases and in time most of the forward centres were closed.

For the soldiers returned to England there was a similar mixture of therapies. Officers may have ended up at Craiglockhart Military Hospital under the care of William Rivers

(1864–1922; FRCP 1899; FRS) where a refined psychoanalytic regime was in place. Most were treated at other centres such as Maghull Hospital in Liverpool; Seale Hayne, a specialist rehabilitation unit for war neuroses staffed by physicians not psychiatrists; and a special hospital for war neuroses in Denmark Hill run by Edward Mapother (1881–1940; FRCP 1927).

Gordon Morgan Holmes was a dominant physician on the Western Front and in the handling of cases of shell shock. He trained at Trinity College Dublin, studied in Frankfurt and around 1900 was offered a post there, but turned it down as he would have had to have assumed German nationality; thus did the British medical war effort have a narrow escape. He was appointed to the National Hospital Queen Square in 1903 as the hospital's first junior house physician and, in 1909,

Shell-shocked soldier, the Battle of the Somme, July–November 1916 (© Imperial War Museum (Q 79508))

Choreic movement disorder in shell shock 1916 (Image courtesy of Army Medical Services Museum)

Lord Moran (1882–1977). Portrait by Pietro Annigoni 1951

There is an unverified story that Churchill said of this famous portrait 'Just right Moran – makes you look like a mediaeval poisoner'

as neurologist to the Hospital. When war was declared in August 1914, he volunteered for service in the RAMC but was rejected because of myopia. He went to France anyway with (Sir) Percy Sargent (1873–1933), a leading Queen Square neurosurgeon, to work in a Red Cross Hospital in the Astoria Hotel in Paris. The War Office, fortunately realising their mistake, ignored his myopia and appointed him consultant to the British Expeditionary Force in France, where he remained until 1918 working largely at Stationary Hospital No. 13 in Boulogne. He was capable of long hours of work, had remarkable powers of observation and concentration, and was tyrannical in an Edwardian manner, likely contributing to his effectiveness. He became embroiled in organising the management of shell shock victims, although he had little sympathy with their plight, which he considered a sign of character weakness. In France, Holmes met Rosalie Jobson (1876–1963), a female medical officer and an Oxford graduate, a hockey international, and later a paediatrician, and proposed to her while rowing on the Thames during their leave. They lived after the war in a large house at 9 Wimpole Street, with nine servants, but Holmes still started each day with a cold bath and washed his thick hair, a habit acquired in France to remove lice.

Charles McMoran Wilson (later Lord Moran) (1882–1977; PRCP 1941–50) was born in Yorkshire and trained at St Mary's Hospital. He was a College mogul (so skilled in negotiations he was later dubbed 'corkscrew Charlie'), elected Treasurer in 1938 and President between 1941 and 1950. He enlisted in 1914 as medical officer in the Royal Fusiliers, won the Military Cross in 1916 during the battle of the Somme and in 1917 took charge of the medical facilities at the British 7th Stationary Hospital in Boulogne. In 1945 he wrote *The Anatomy of Courage*, a story of heroism and tragedy in which Moran wrote that war accounted for his 'loss of faith in the infallibility of authority'. He discusses the role of fear and the importance of leadership for maintaining morale in his book, and for many years lectured on courage at the Staff College at Camberley. He recognised the dangers of shell shock for the war effort and viewed it as a form of degeneracy, linked to urbanisation:

Such men went about plainly unable to stand this test of men [war]. They had about them the marks known to our calling of the incomplete man, the stamp of degeneracy ... just a worthless chap, without shame, the worst product of the towns ... [sent to] a shell shock hospital with a rabble of mis-shapen creatures from the towns.

William Aldren Turner (1864–1945; FRCP 1896) was another neurologist sent to France in 1914 to investigate shell shock. In meetings with Gordon Holmes and Charles Myers, he dictated the strategy and organisation for dealing with these cases. In December 1914, he persuaded the Chairman of the National Hospital Queen Square to set apart wards entirely for the treatment of nervous shock and, of the 1,272 soldiers treated at the hospital during the war, 462 had no identifiable organic pathology and most of these cases were of 'shell shock'. After the war, Turner was one of the sixteen appointed members of the War Office Committee of Enquiry into Shell Shock which produced its celebrated report in 1922.

Lewis Ralph Yealland (1885–1954; FRCP 1937) was a Canadian who during World War I was appointed resident medical officer and then registrar at the National Hospital Queen Square. He worked with E.D. Adrian (Lord Adrian; 1889–1977; FRCP 1924; FRS. Adrian later won the 1932 Nobel Prize in Physiology or Medicine, jointly with Sir

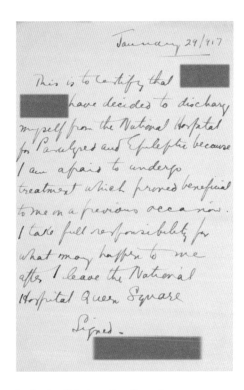

A patient's self-discharge from Queen Square and the care of Dr Yealland – fearing repetition of his previous therapy 1917 (Image courtesy of the Queen Square Library, Archive and Museum)

Charles Sherrington (1857–1952; FRCP 1912; FRS), for his neurophysiological work and the first recording of electrical action potentials in nerves). They initiated an infamous treatment regimen for shell shock there in 1915, which is described in detail in Yealland's book *Hysterical Disorders of Warfare*. Yealland gained later notoriety as a chief protagonist in Pat Barker's prizewinning trilogy *Regeneration*. The depiction of Yealland as a doctor basing his treatment on punishment by electrical shock does not accord with contemporary sources, which show him more a compassionate and kindly individual.

He took the view that shell shock was best managed by techniques based on persuasion and suggestion. He elected to use the term 'functional nervous disorder' rather than hysteria and explained the soldiers' handicaps in physical terms to avoid giving the impression that he considered them to be malingerers. However, his treatment methods were of their time, and would be highly questionable today. He adopted an authoritative manner and appealed to the serviceman's sense of honour and familial responsibility: 'if you recover quickly, then it is due to a disease, if you recover slowly … then I shall decide that your condition is due to malingering'. Any method of counter-suggestion could be used, provided that it was strong enough to persuade the patient that he could be cured. The preferred method of therapy was 'suggestive treatment and re-education', including applying a faradic current to dysfunctional parts at increasing strengths, sometimes until the pain was unbearable, and an authoritarian and overbearing attitude to overawe the soldiers. For functional deafness tuning forks of different frequencies were applied to the mastoid. Occasionally an electrical current was applied to the scalp overlying the motor cortex, as in the case of an officer who had some knowledge of neuro-anatomy, who recovered promptly. Yealland emphasised that the therapy had to be delivered by a physician brimful with confidence, outwardly bored by having to cure yet another hysteric with faradism, and adopting an air of complete assurance rather than offering explanation. 'As soon as the least sign of recovery has appeared … the patient is given no time to collect his thoughts … is never allowed any say in the matter … but is hurried along … until the disordered function has completely recovered'.

'Now look, men...there may be a god up there, or then again there may not be, but assuming for the moment that there is, then I'm pretty sure he's on our side'

Cartoon from Punch 1990 (© Punch Limited)

Yealland treated at least 196 soldiers admitted to Queen Square claiming recovery in eighty-eight, improvement in eighty-four and failure in twenty-four, but conceded his method often did not produce a permanent cure and relapse was highly probable. Relatively few soldiers returned to the Front. No doubt fear of electrocution filled some of the soldiers with dread, forcing them to take their own discharge, while the prospect of painful treatment led to a 'miraculous spontaneous recovery' in others. The Matron of the hospital reported to the Hospital Secretary one morning that 'the fish was bad again yesterday and one of the soldiers hung himself in the stable'.

Dudley William Carmalt-Jones (1874–1957; FRCP 1914) served in France from 1914, initially at No. 14 Stationary Hospital in the Hotel Splendide (officers) and Casino (ranks) at Wimereux. In January 1917 he was put in charge of the shell shock centre at No. 4 Stationary Hospital at Arques. His descriptions, published in *Brain* in 1919, are based on his experience of 4,700 cases attending the centre and his statistical analysis of the 1,300 he examined in most detail. His autobiography, *A Physician in Spite of Himself*, was published in 2009 but interestingly has little information about his work with shell shock, perhaps an example of how many tried to forget this whole medical episode.

MISSILE INJURY TO THE HEAD

Gordon Holmes and his neurosurgical colleague Percy Sargent were, in Hospital No. 13 in Boulogne, also deeply involved in dealing with missile injuries to the head. Neurosurgical techniques advanced enormously, initially with the research of Sir Victor Horsley (1857–1916; FRS), who studied bullet wounds on experimental animals and evolved procedures for dealing with head injury that were remarkably effective in this pre-antibiotic era. These included early operation, removal of all shrapnel and foreign bodies, and meticulous debridement. A new type of injury was the 'gutter injury' caused by bullets traversing the skull of unfortunate soldiers poking their heads above the trenches. It seems this caused sinus thrombosis, the victim often rendered immediately quadriplegic, but remarkably making a full recovery over weeks if managed properly.

The massive influx of cases of head injury presented an opportunity for medical discovery. And so it was, with the aid of war, that Gordon Holmes made brilliant observations of the effects of injury to the occipital cortex and cerebellum. This work was made possible by the poor design of the British Army helmet, leaving the back of the head exposed. These observations formed the basis of his classic work on the cerebellum and the cerebral anatomy of vision. Holmes worked until 5am in freezing hospital environments, dressed in his British Warm (overcoat), wrapped in a rug and with his hands in mittens, while carrying out studies on visual localisation. He had little equipment and wrote up his own notes. The American neurosurgeon Harvey Cushing, visiting in 1916 was astounded by the quality of work done under such primitive and overwhelming conditions:

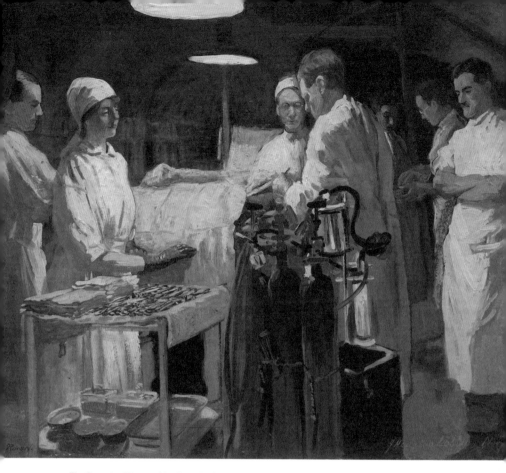

The Operating Theatre, 41st Casualty Clearing Station. J. Hodgson Lobley 1918 (© Imperial War Museum (ART 3750))

After Tea, Holmes and Sargent took me back to No. 13, where I saw an amazing number of head and spinal wounds, for they often received daily convoys of 300 recently wounded. With the proper backing these two men have an unparalleled opportunity, not only to be of service to the individual wounded, but, when this is all over, to make a contribution to physiology, neurology and surgery which will be epochal ... On the whole, I take No. 13 to be a good example of the large overseas hospitals of the RAMC. The comforts are slight, the attendance insufficient, the work, though it naturally varies, is simply overwhelming – perhaps as many admissions in a day as the American Ambulance might get in a month ... This is truly a man-sized job, in the midst of which the Britisher stops for tea, and everyone – even down to the Tommie – has time to shave; and its taking-it-quietly that possibly enables them to see things through with some measure of composure.

Another early description of Hospital No. 13 is given by A.L. Walker, a Red Cross nurse arriving in Boulogne on 30 October 1914:

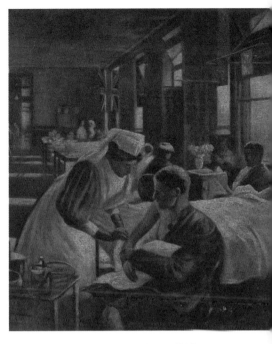

The first wounded, London Hospital, August 1914.
Sir John Lavery 1914 (Wellcome Library, London)

The place gave us the impression of being a seething mass of ambulances, wounded men, doctors and nurses: there seemed to be an unending stream of each of them. All the hotels were hospitals, which gave one a horrid feeling of disaster ... The sugar sheds on the Gare Maritime were to be converted into a hospital, No. 13 Stationary Hospital. What an indescribable scene! In the first huge shed there were hundreds of wounded walking cases (as long as a man could crawl he had to be a walking case). All were caked with mud, in torn clothes, hardly any caps, and with blood-stained bandages on arms, hands, and legs; many were lying asleep on the straw that had been left in the hastily cleaned sheds, looking weary to death; others sitting on empty boxes or barrels, eating the contents of a tin of 'Maconochie' with the help of a clasp knife. Dressings were being carried out on improvised tables; blood-stained clothes, caked in mud, which had been cut off, were stacked in heaps with rifles and ammunition. Further on, the sheds were being converted into wards; wooden partitions were being run up, bedsteads carried in, the wounded meanwhile lying about on straw or stretchers. The beds were for stretcher cases, and were soon filled with terribly wounded men, who had just to be put into the beds as they were, clothes and all. As fast as one could get to them the clothes were cut off, the patient washed and his wounds dressed. Some had both legs off, some their side blown away – all were wounded in several places. Doctors and nurses were hopelessly outnumbered, distractedly endeavouring to meet the demands made upon them. Here too we found the Matron-in-Chief with the Expeditionary Force in France [Dame Maud McCarthy] helping and directing. Under her supervision a miraculous change soon took place; reinforcements of nurses began to arrive, and the sheds took on the appearance of a well ordered hospital.

GAS WARFARE

Indian soldiers in Dome, Brighton. Douglas Fox-Pitt 1919 (© Imperial War Museum (ART 323))

The Hague Conventions of 1899 and 1907 prohibited the use of chemical weapons and, although signed by the Allies and by Germany, this did not stop large-scale chemical use for the first time in the history of warfare in World War I. Initial trials of xylyl bromide were made by the German Army on the Eastern Front in 1915, but chlorine was then chosen as the favoured weapon. It was first used in the Second Battle of Ypres, a town which became known as the City of Gas, on the afternoon of 22 April 1915. Based on meteorological reports of favourable winds, a special unit of the German Army released 168 tonnes of chlorine gas (Cl_2) toward the British and French trenches from 6,000 steel cylinders placed along their lines. The gas formed a great grey-green cloud drifting into the British trenches and caused mayhem. On Hill 60, it is recorded that ninety men died in the trenches in the first attack, and of the 207 reaching dressing stations, forty-six died almost immediately and twelve after long suffering. Over the next weeks further attacks were made; war had entered a new phase. The medical effects were predominantly in the lungs, where 1,000 parts per million will destroy alveolar tissue, and in the eyes. The chemists were impressed and intense research into more lethal agents was undertaken on both sides.

The next gas used, in 1915, was phosgene (carbonyl chloride ($COCl_2$)) sometimes mixed with chlorine and then, in July 1917, mustard gas ($\beta\beta'$-dichlorethyl ($ClCH_2CH_2)_2S$) which was the most effective of all. The mustards

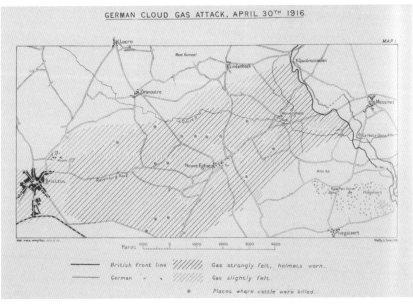

TOP: Gas cloud on the battlefield at Ypres (Courtesy of National Archives (111-SC-10879))
ABOVE: Map of German gas attacks 30 April 1916 (Wellcome Library, London)

Gassed – In arduis fidelis. Gilbert Rogers 1919 (© Imperial War Museum (ART 3819))

were developed in Germany and were dispatched in artillery shells, where they formed oily patches on the ground which remained active for days or weeks. The poison was absorbed through the skin, causing intense translucent, yellowish blistering, which could advance to necrosis. It affected the airways, in severe cases resulting in asphyxiation and pulmonary oedema, and the eyes, causing conjunctivitis and in severe cases corneal damage. The effects were slow and progressive and death was often protracted, sometimes taking weeks of agony. Among the survivors, because of the alkylation of DNA, carcinogenesis was a further risk. A total of 160,000 British chemical casualties were caused by mustard gas with a death toll of 2.6 per cent due to respiratory failure or superadded sepsis. By the end of the war, 190,000 tons of chemicals had been used by all sides. Mustard was known as the 'king of the battle gases' as it caused more casualties than all other chemical agents combined – but even then the numbers killed by gas were relatively small compared to the overall slaughter of the war.

Gas, however, had a further dimension. It induced a great sense of fear that many soldiers felt was worse than that of shelling, and 'gas shock' matched 'shell shock' in its psychological effects. Gas eroded self-control and raised the terrifying spectre of suffocation. Alfred Bertram Soltau (1876–1930; FRCP 1925) examined the files of 150 soldiers given an invalidity pension due to gassing and found that thirty per cent reported symptoms which would have met the criteria for neurasthenia, or shell shock,

ABOVE: World War I gas masks (Francis Whiting Halsey)
PAGES OVERLEAF: *Ypres, 1915.* Gilbert Rogers 1919 (© Imperial War Museum (ART 3792))

and another twenty-five per cent the psychosomatic condition of 'soldier's heart'. Soltau had been placed in command of the 2nd Wessex Field Ambulance and in 1916 he was made consulting physician to the First and Second Armies, where he became responsible for advice regarding gas attacks. He devised treatment and management procedures, and recognised that the psychological effects and fear of being gassed were often as bad as the physical effects – 'there is nothing probably more liable to cause panic than the idea of being choked … the dread of being slowly strangled'. He was heavily decorated for his contributions and in addition to his British honours was awarded the Croix de Guerre in 1918.

As chlorine, the first gas used on an industrial scale, is very water soluble, covering the mouth with gauze soaked in bicarbonate solution was thought to protect the lungs and a campaign was started in the British press asking women to make cotton pads to send to the Front. These measures proved not very effective as the soldiers found it difficult to breathe through the wet pads, but by July 1915 the British Medical Corps had been issued with a 'hypo helmet' – a wool hood with a mica window. This was followed by the 'PH' helmet in which air was inhaled and exhaled through the fabric. It incorporated an expiratory valve, and the cloth was then impregnated with chemicals designed to destroy phosgene. It was stiflingly hot and prolonged wear resulted in carbon dioxide retention. In 1916, small box respirators were in production and these provided the first really useful protection from the various chemical agents used. Soldiers kept their masks beside them and donned their hoods or masks whenever the alarm was sounded.

The medical treatment of an exposed soldier differed according to the agent. Soldiers afflicted by chlorine and phosgene were evacuated and treated with oxygen and rest until they were healthy enough to return to the Front. Soldiers exposed to mustard gas

needed immediate washing of the eyes and skin. Decontamination within a few minutes of exposure was the only effective means of preventing tissue damage, and so had to be performed by the soldier. Showering to remove the agent from the skin was carried out on the Western Front in special bath trucks with a hot-water boiler and fold-down shower heads deployed behind the lines, but in actuality, by the time a shower was taken the mustard had usually been absorbed and skin decontamination was fruitless. Victims were then issued new uniforms and their clothing was decontaminated and reissued. The severe cases were evacuated and lung, skin and eye care was instituted depending on the severity of the case. No medicinal products were available to counter the effects of gas, and the unfortunate victims of all types had simply to rest and receive supportive measures. The average recuperation time from mustard gas and phosgene was around seven weeks and then the soldiers were returned to the Front.

Unlike most of the military fellows, Sir Alfred Keogh was a career army soldier, joining up in 1892, serving in the Boer War and, in 1905, appointed Director-General of the Army Medical Services (DGAMS). He retired in 1910, but with the outbreak of war was reappointed. Onto his shoulders was placed the task of rapidly organising the necessary massive expansion of medical facilities for the war. He was a born organiser. *The Spectator* noted:

> *... the vast and complex service of doctors, ambulances, dressing-stations, hospitals, and sanitary experts which has kept the Army remarkably free from disease, has spared the wounded all needless pain, and has reduced the mortality from wounds or sickness to a degree that would have seemed incredibly low to our fathers ... and millions of sick and wounded men have reason to bless his name.*

OPPOSITE: Navy gas
mask on *HMS Warrior*
Hospital Ship 1919
(Wellcome Library, London)
ABOVE: *Gassed at Estaires
1918 (*© Imperial War
Museum (Q 11586))
RIGHT: *Sir Alfred Keogh.*
Arthur Hacker (Image
courtesy of Army Medical
Services Museum, with
permission of the Royal
Army Medical Corps
Collection)

British anti-gas 'respirator' 1915 (© Imperial War Museum (EQU 3906_1_A and EQU 3906_1_C))

Before the war, Keogh had been appointed Rector of Imperial College and it was his colleagues there, Herbert Baker and J. S. Haldane, who visited the front line at Ypres in April 1915 with him and identified chlorine as the first gas used in warfare. Haldane's and Baker's passports had to be issued with such speed that there was no time to develop a photograph and a thumb print was used instead. Haldane is said to have recognised the gas as chlorine from the tarnishing of brass buttons, and he and Baker then tested the first helmets on themselves in a gas chamber; Haldane it is said suffered worse. Baker continued to work on respirator design and these saved thousands of lives. Keogh must have had great charm as he was greatly respected by the French and had perfected the art of persuading aristocratic ladies to give up their stately homes for hospitals. He was the first army physician to be elevated to the Knight Grand Cross of the Order of the Bath and received many other honours including the splendidly named award of the Order of the White Eagle (Second Class) by the equally splendid King of Serbia, and election as Grand Officer of the Legion of Honour by the President of France.

DISEASE NOMENCLATURE

The publication in 1869 of the College's *Nomenclature of diseases* created an international standard for the classification of diseases, which was to last through five editions until the twentieth century. The RCP nomenclature of disease was adopted by the War Office, but advances in knowledge and the appearance of new conditions led the latter to express concern about some of the definitions.

The Government's Medical Research Committee (MRC), the forerunner of the present Medical Research Council, pursued the arguments on behalf of the War Office in a letter to Dr Guthrie on 13 January 1917, concerned particularly with definitions of two diseases rife at the Front – jaundice and shell shock.

The MRC urged the College to abandon its plans to introduce the terms 'epidemic jaundice' and 'Weil's disease', and to substitute 'spirochaetal jaundice' for the latter. The Committee commented 'there is little justification for the perpetual commemoration of Weil'. They reflected here the views of Bertrand Dawson PRCP (later Viscount Dawson of Penn) that the term Weil's disease:

... is not justified by the facts. The condition had been described by the French under the more comprehensive title of 'Infectious Jaundice' prior to the publication of Weil's cases. Weil ignored the French work and on the basis of a few cases attached his own name to the condition.

The MRC preferred infectious jaundice, or post-catarrhal jaundice, for non-spirochaetal disease. In reply the College expressed its wish to maintain Weil's disease in the nomenclature, but the MRC urged reconsideration: 'Very many will think it unfortunate that a particular German should be commemorated in connection with a disease he was not the first to describe. I understand that the French physicians feel this very strongly.'

The MRC was not impressed by the PRCP's suggestion of '*spirochaetosis icterohaemorrhagica*' which they dismissed as:

... conferring no advantage whatever in clarity or usefulness, and on the other hand to inflict the most grievous burden upon every unfortunate medical officer, registrar

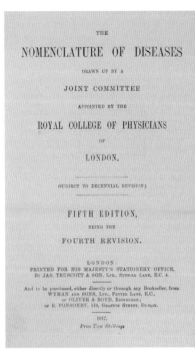

THE

NOMENCLATURE OF DISEASES

DRAWN UP BY A

JOINT COMMITTEE

APPOINTED BY THE

ROYAL COLLEGE OF PHYSICIANS

OF

LONDON.

(SUBJECT TO DECENNIAL REVISION)

FIFTH EDITION,

BEING THE

FOURTH REVISION.

LONDON
PRINTED FOR HIS MAJESTY'S STATIONERY OFFICE,
BY JAS. TRUSCOTT & SON, LTD, SUFFOLK LANE, E.C. 4.

And to be purchased, either directly or through any Bookseller, from
WYMAN AND SONS, LTD., FETTER LANE, E.C.,
or OLIVER & BOYD, EDINBURGH;
or E. PONSONBY, 116, GRAFTON STREET, DUBLIN.

1917.

Price Two Shillings

Title page, 5th edition of *The Nomenclature of Diseases* 1917 (Photography Mike Fear)

or orderly who might have to write those dreadful words upon cramped official forms. Suffering human nature would instantly contrive some slang corruption.

The War Office also found difficulties with the term shell shock, which they wished to have divided into 'shell concussion (with evidence of actual physical agitation), and shell neurasthenia'. The MRC pointed out that lack of official recognition of the latter might lead to unfair descriptions of cowardice or malingering. The College responded with the suggestion of 'Neurasthenia, traumatic, including the effects of shell exposure unaccompanied by concussion'. In the eventuality, the recommendations on shell shock were accepted. Weil's disease was dropped (though not suppressed for ever!) and the unwieldy *spirochaetosis icterohaemorrhagica* survived.

```
                                          14 General Hospital,
                                          France. B.E.F.

                                          December 30th 1916.

Dear Sir Alfred,

        Elliott told me this afternoon that on the advice of the
College of Physicians the War Office is about to adopt in the
matter of jaundice the terms "Weil's Disease" and "Epidemic
Jaundice".
        I would urge that the best term is "Infective Jaundice".
Then where the cause of the infection is known the qualificat-
ion can be added thus:-
                          Enteric Infective Jaundice.
                          Spirochaetal Infective Jaundice.
                          Pneumococcal        do         do
                          Streptococcal       do         do
or, if preferred, the qualifying term can be put in brackets
after Infective Jaundice, e.g. "Infective Jaundice (Spirochae-
tal)".
        If, in any case, the infective agent were not known the
illness would be styled simply "Infective Jaundice".
        Whether these varieties of jaundice are epidemic or not
depends on circumstances.
        The term "Weil's Disease" is not justified by the facts.
The condition had been described by the French under the more
comprehensive title of "Infectious Jaundice" prior to the pub-
lication of Weil's cases. Weil ignored the French work and on
the basis of a few cases attached his own name to the condition.
As time has gone by the term "Weil's Disease" has been in-
creasingly employed to denote any form if Infectious Jaundice
with fever. As a consequence confusion results and doubtless
Typhoid and Paratyphoid Fever have been thus disguised.
        We have urged this point of view in our article on
jaundice, the appearance of which in the "Quarterly Journal of
Medicine" keeps constantly being postponed because the
Military Authorities have combed out all the colour block
makers.

                          Yours sincerely,

                          (Signed)  Bertrand Dawson.
```

Letter from Bertrand (later Lord) Dawson on appropriate nomenclature for Infectious Jaundice 1916 (Photography Mike Fear)

Stationary Hospital no. 2, France 1918 (Image courtesy of Army Medical Services Museum)

WORLD WAR II

World War I had eclipsed all previous conflicts in terms of death and injury. It is estimated that ten million persons died and twenty million were wounded. Destruction on a scale not previously contemplated had occurred and the dire effects of the mechanisation of war had shocked all at the time. In the words of Woodrow Wilson, it was 'the war to end all wars', and this indeed was the hope of many over the next decade. However, this was not to be so – World War II was even more devastating. It was a global conflict involving most nations of the world and it has been suggested that seventy-five million people died, including twenty million military personnel. Although World War II posed huge challenges to the medical authorities, and to physicians, as in World War I, adversity spawned innovation. New diseases were described, organisation of care was transformed and novel treatments were developed, for instance in the fields of antibiotics, vaccines, blood transfusion, kidney disease, injuries and rehabilitation.

THE COLLEGE IN WORLD WAR II

The war also changed the College. In the pre-war period, perhaps because of the influence of Lord Dawson (1864–1945; PRCP 1931–37), the RCP began to engage more in wider international affairs, externally expressing support, for instance, for the League of Nations on disarmament and for a protest against the treatment of the Jews in Nazi Germany (although Dawson and the College placed many bars to the emigration of doctors from Germany to Britain during the 1930s). Domestically, the College started taking a generally progressive view on such topics as birth control, sexual relations and eugenics. Dawson had a good war record in World War I, was mentioned in despatches and subsequently chaired the Army Medical Board, but is best remembered for the Dawson Report of 1920 on the provision of health services, which was a landmark in the refashioning of the profession in the modern world and contained recommendations which were influential in the formation of the NHS.

However, in respect of the war effort, the RCP as an institution was, as in the first war, to a great extent inert. In 1938, Sir Robert Hutchison (1871–1960; PRCP 1938–41) was elected President and in fact even suggested that the College should be closed down for the duration of the war, a suggestion fiercely opposed by the younger fellows appalled by the lack of College involvement in military medical affairs, in strong contrast, for instance, to the contribution of the British Medical Association. A more robust line was taken by Dr Charles Wilson (Lord Moran), who succeeded Hutchison as PRCP in 1941, although even then throughout the war the College's contribution remained limited.

In 1939, the College Council had been designated the Emergency War Committee, but remarkably few specifically war-related issues were debated. Most interwar

OPPOSITE: *Dunkirk: Embarkation of wounded.* Edward Bawden, May 1940 (© Imperial War Museum (ART LD 177))

Bomb-damaged roof, Royal College of Physicians, Pall Mall, November 1940

discussion was about examinations, complaints about the treatment of the doctors by the new Emergency Medical Service (EMS), then the Goodenough Interdepartmental Report into Medical Education, and above all else the spectre of the rise of state medicine.

The College buildings in Pall Mall were hit by bombs in the blitz of October and November 1940, the latter attack destroying most of the roof. The treasures and books from the library were evacuated and dispersed to various locations.

A most significant outcome of the war, from the College point of view, was the appetite among the British people to set up a state medical service, which took shape in the form of the NHS. The College initially took up a hostile and opposing view and in 1942, for instance, the Council expressed its opposition to a: 'State medical Service in the sense of a whole time salaried Government

Service for the whole of the profession providing all the necessary medical services for the whole community'. In 1944, it recorded a view that the:

... new relationship which will result from the sudden and considerable increase in salaried medical practice is contrary to the tradition of the medical profession. For the sake of the people it is a matter of urgency that the quality of medical service should be preserved, and the practice of medicine as a free and liberal profession should be safeguarded.

Eventually though, bowing to the inevitable, it fell in step with the plans of the post-war Labour government.

On 2 March 1944, the College entertained the Prime Minister Winston Churchill to Luncheon at the Savoy Hotel – Lobster Mousseline, Roast Turkey and Fruit Salad were on the menu. This was a landmark meeting which 222 fellows and fifty-eight guests attended. Moran gave an address drawing attention to the similarities between the professions of medicine and the military, but stressing the importance of the emphasis on research and independence of thought in medicine. In Moran's view, both medicine and the military needed one utterly essential feature among their practitioners – character. He ended with a fulsome tribute to Churchill, who responded:

Our policy is to create a national health service in order to ensure that everybody in the country, irrespective of means, age, sex, or occupation, shall have equal opportunities to benefit from the best and most up-to-date medical and allied services available. The plan that we have put forward is a very large-scale plan, and in ordinary times of peace would rivet and dominate the attention of the whole country; but even during this war it deserves the close study and thought of all who can spare themselves from other duties for that purpose. We welcome constructive criticism; we claim the loyal and active aid of the whole medical profession.

He welcomed science:

The destiny of our country, which after all has rendered notable services to mankind in peace and latterly in war, depends upon an ever-flowing fountain of healthy children, born into what we trust will be a broader society and a less distracted world. Science, now so largely perverted to destruction, must raise its glittering shield not only over the children but over the mothers, not only over the family but over the home. In all this field again you must be active. Your services will be given with devotion and your voice will be heard with respect.

He ended his speech in true Churchillian fashion:

This College must play its part in keeping alive the historic tradition of the medical profession, and must ever foster those high standards of professional behaviour which distinguish a profession from a trade. This is what you have tried to do as an institution for 400 years. I confess myself to be a great admirer of tradition. The longer you can look back the further you can look forward. The wider the span, the longer the continuity, the greater is the sense of duty in individual men and women, each contributing their brief life's work to the preservation and progress of the land in which they live, of the society of which they are members, and the world of which they are the servants.

The College may not have been central to the war effort, but its fellows and members in their other capacities were active in many fields. To an extent, greater than ever before, medicine made a profound difference to the outcome of the wounded and in its turn the war also irreversibly changed medicine.

THE EMERGENCY MEDICAL SERVICE

One extraordinary feature, in marked contrast to the chaotic situation in World War I, was the greatly improved organisation of medical services both in the theatres of war but particularly on the Home Front and especially in London. Much had been learned from World War I and the country was, from the medical point of view, in a much better state of readiness, in large part due to the efforts of a small number of physicians. The EMS was a good example. This was mandated by central government to deploy the medical services in London in a coordinated and rational manner – of course a total contrast to the patchwork arrangements of peacetime London – and the Emergency Powers Act allowed the Ministry of Health to issue formal directions to all hospitals, including the voluntary hospitals which were not hitherto susceptible to state control.

The main reason for the scheme was the prediction that, within two weeks of the declaration of war, 100,000 bombs would be dropped over London and 320,000 casualties were anticipated. The bombardment fortunately did not happen as early as expected and the delay allowed the arrangements that had initially lagged behind to take full effect. However, in June 1940 air raids over London did begin, and by September 1940 these had become extremely heavy and remained so until May 1941. In that period of the Blitz 46,518 bombs were dropped on London, 29,120 people were killed and 47,046 were detained in hospital.

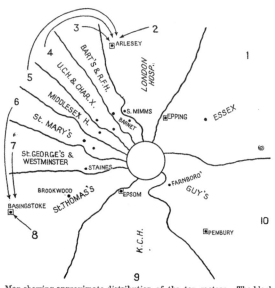

Proposed distribution of Emergency Medical Services, London. Lancet 1939 (Reprinted from The Lancet, Hospitals in emergency the scheme for London; 233:723–725. Copyright (1939), with permission from Elsevier Ltd)

Map showing approximate distribution of the ten sectors. The black circles show the position of advance-base hospitals; the circles in squares are the base hospitals.

TOP: Two German Dornier bombers over south-east London. 7 September 1940 (© Imperial War Museum (C 5424))
ABOVE LEFT: Tube station shelter, Elephant and Castle. Bill Brandt November 1940 (© Imperial War Museum (D 1572))
ABOVE RIGHT: Homeless. Clifford Hall 1940 (© Imperial War Museum (ART LD 788))

In that period of the Blitz, 46,518 bombs were dropped on London, 29,120 people were killed and 47,046 were detained in hospital.

X-ray department, Queen Alexandra Military Hospital.
Frances Macdonald 1941 (© Imperial War Museum
(ART LD 791))

The EMS became in effect the midwife at the birth, a decade later, of the NHS.

In the EMS scheme, the 2,378 London hospitals were organised into ten sections. One central hospital (usually the well-established large teaching hospital) was designed to act for the immediate admission of patients who would then be evacuated as quickly as possible to the hospitals on the periphery. Other 'Class 1' hospitals in the inner zone would be allowed to admit the sick and casualties but most hospitals were given a subsidiary role. Hospital blocks of 300 or more beds were allotted for military purposes and an ambulance service was set up to move patients around through the system. Within a few days of the outbreak of war, the first emergency order was issued, requiring the evacuation of as many patients as possible from inner London. Within a week, 56,000 patients had been moved out of the inner London hospitals, along with much of their medical equipment. Emergency pathology and blood transfusion services were set up, as were special centres for orthopaedic injury, head injury, plastic surgery, burns, chest and maxillary-facial injury. Whole teams of surgeons were redeployed to

the periphery of London – for instance the neurosurgeons at the National Hospital Queen Square, who were moved to set up a new neurosurgical facility in Hayward's Heath and a new head injury unit at Leavesden Hospital. The scheme ran remarkably smoothly and was highly admired. It most importantly provided proof of principle, in the mind of the British public, that central state control of medicine had many advantages. The EMS became in effect the midwife at the birth, a decade later, of the NHS.

Lord Moran was in charge of one large sector of the EMS but, in practice, most of his time was taken up as physician to Sir Winston Churchill. An important figure was George Riddoch (1888–1947; FRCP 1925), who was in charge of the EMS neurological unit and Consulting Neurologist to the Army. He had had a distinguished career researching spinal injuries in World War I and when war was joined again, there seemed to be hardly a committee concerned with medical services on which he did not sit. He chaired the MRC Peripheral Nerve Injury Committee, which in 1943 drafted the famous MRC booklet on the *Investigation of peripheral nerve injuries* (this is still in use today in its sixth edition). It was also Riddoch who was instrumental in establishing the group in Oxford at St Hugh's, which was to prove so influential to neurology and neurosurgery. When he died at the age of fifty-eight, in the aftermath of surgery for a peptic ulcer, his death was widely attributed to massive overwork.

LEFT: *St. Clement Dane's church on fire after being bombed.* Henry Carr 1941 (© Imperial War Museum (ART LD 1315))
BELOW: Blitz damage, Paternoster Square on 29 December 1941 (© Imperial War Museum (HU 108965))

NEW MEDICAL TREATMENTS AND DISEASES IN WORLD WAR II

One discovery which had a profound effect on wartime medicine was that of penicillin. The antibiotic effect was first identified in September 1928 by Alexander Fleming (1881–1955; FRCP 1944; FRS), bacteriologist at St Mary's Hospital in London, who noted that the growth of colonies of *Staphylococcus aureus* in a petri dish left by chance on his desk was inhibited by a contaminating fungus, *Penicillium notatum*. He further experimented with penicillin as an antiseptic but seems rather to have overlooked its potential as an antibiotic drug. It was the work of the Oxford group on germicides, funded by the MRC and the Rockefeller Foundation, which first realised the potential of penicillin. In 1938, Howard Florey (1898–1968; FRCP 1951; FRS), Professor of Pathology and Director of the Sir William Dunn School of Pathology at Oxford University, began his work which led to the isolation and purification of the active ingredient of the mould. The experiments were carried out with his brilliant junior biochemist, the German Jewish refugee Sir Ernst Chain (1906–79; FRCP 1965; FRS), and on Saturday 25 May 1940 enough penicillin had been produced for the first *in vivo* experiment. It was injected into mice with overwhelming sepsis and they recovered. The first human treatment was in 1941 ('penicillin grown in chamber pots and purified by passage through the Oxford police force') and the first conclusive clinical trial, in 187 cases, was carried out in 1942. In the summer of 1943 Florey and the Oxford neurosurgeon Hugh Cairns went to North Africa and experimented successfully with using penicillin in war wounds.

Florey failed initially to persuade the British pharmaceutical industry, over-encumbered by the war and war damage, to produce penicillin and so Florey and Chain, and their assistant Norman Heatley, turned their department into a small factory producing, in true British Heath Robinson fashion, penicillium mould culture fluid extracts. Their makeshift methods were insufficient to produce enough antibiotic to use in man and, with the approval of the MRC, Florey handed his information to scientists in the USA. A rather unfortunate takeover by American pharmaceutical companies began and although by 1942 the drug was in production in Britain and America, the Americans had patented a method of deep fermentation at a time when it was not usual practice to patent discoveries in medical research. Florey was criticised for giving away valuable commercial assets, and penicillin, like the CT scanner and monoclonal antibodies, became an example of the narrative of great British medical discoveries exploited commercially elsewhere. By 1942, industrial production was well underway and by the end of the war 650 billion units a month were being produced. Fleming, Florey and Chain won the Nobel Prize in Physiology or Medicine in 1945.

Penicillin was, however, not the first antibiotic. The credit for this goes to Sir Lionel Ernest Howard Whitby (1895–1956; FRCP 1933), Professor of Physic at Cambridge

RIGHT: Sir Ernst Chain
at the Sir William Dunn
School of Pathology,
Oxford (© Imperial War
Museum (TR 1458))
BELOW: *Early penicillin
culture vessels.* Harold
Axtell c1950 (Museum
of the History of Science,
University of Oxford)

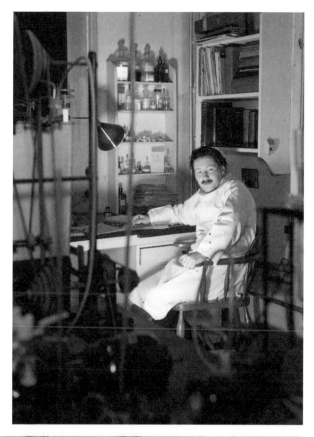

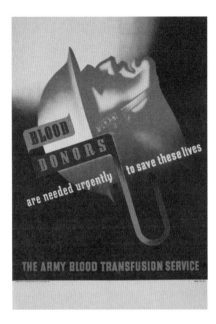

Army blood transfusion services poster, World War II
(Wellcome Library, London)

University. He had won an MC in
World War I during Passchendaele,
but was later wounded and had a leg
amputated in 1918, which ended his
career in the army. He then studied
medicine in Cambridge and, as Assistant
Pathologist at the Middlesex Hospital,
began to research sulphonamide
compounds. With Arthur Ewins, from the
British pharmaceutical company May
and Baker Ltd, Whitby identified the
benefits of sulphapyridine and this was
manufactured as 'M&B 693'. It was first
used clinically in 1938 and widely by
the military during the war before being
superseded by penicillin.

Whitby's contribution to the war effort,
though, was not limited to antibiotics.
In World War II, he was appointed as
the first officer in charge of the Army
Blood Transfusion Service and became

responsible for the efficient organisation
of this service. Stationed in Bristol, he
managed to establish, despite heavy
German bombing, the army blood
supply depot and a school for training
transfusion units. His work was widely
admired and became a model for later
peacetime services. During World War
I blood transfusion had been carried
out by direct person-to-person transfer.
The first blood bank was established
in 1917 using sodium citrate to prevent
blood coagulation, and blood could then
be kept on ice, albeit for a short time
only. In 1939, four centres in London
were set up for the storage of blood
in anticipation of an immediate 'blitz'.
John Loutit (1910–92; FRCP 1955),
an Australian Rhodes Scholar, was
appointed as Director of the South
West London Blood Supply Depot at
Sutton, Surrey, and after the war had a
brilliant career in atomic energy. Patrick
Mollison (1914–2011; FRCP 1955)
was seconded, almost at random, to the
same Depot to improve the prospects of
building up stocks of blood. As he wrote:
'The generally used preservative was a
mixture of trisodium citrate and dextrose.
The glucose was autoclaved separately
and added to the citrate after it had
been autoclaved, severe caramelisation
occurred.' By acidifying the preservative,
the volume of anticoagulant – something
like double the volume of blood – could
be dramatically reduced and separate
autoclaving of glucose was unnecessary.
Mollison's recipe (known as ACD)
allowed preservation for up to thirty
(rather than three) days and the process
was used worldwide for the next thirty
years.

The war also saw the first full-scale
investigation into malarial prophylaxis and

ABOVE: Army blood transfusion ambulance – Normandy 1944 (© Imperial War Museum (B 6954)) LEFT: Army blood transfusion service – Fiji (© Imperial War Museum (NZ 1445))

treatment. (Sir) Neil Hamilton Fairley (1891–1966; FRCP 1928) had already established a distinguished record in World War I and the interwar years, and in World War II carefully and systematically researched various antimalarials and proved the effectiveness of mepacrine. Fairley convinced the authorities of its value and orders were then issued that all troops in the Pacific, Indian and Burmese theatres of war were to be given one tablet a day. The rates of malaria fell dramatically – the victory of the land forces in the latter part of the war in the East is sometimes largely ascribed to this single intervention.

Another important success for World War II medicine was the widespread adoption of tetanus toxoid vaccine. This had first been developed in 1924 but was first widely deployed as DTP (diphtheria, tetanus and pertussis) vaccine in World War II. (Sir) John Smith Knox Boyd (1891–1991; FRCP 1951) had an illustrious career in the RAMC in World War I, spent much of the interwar years in India and with the Millbank RAM College, and also worked with the Wellcome company to develop and deploy tetanus vaccine. It is said to be due to his work that tetanus was not a problem in the British army in World War II. Similarly, in the US army as a result of routine vaccination, only twelve tetanus cases were recorded among the 2.7 million soldiers with wounds treated in the army hospitals (and of these six were unvaccinated), a rate one thirtieth of that in World War I.

Another important successfor World War II medicine was the widespread adoption of tetanus toxoid vaccine.

In 1939, Boyd was put in charge of the RAMC vaccine department, which remarkably produced sufficient vaccines for all the service needs throughout the war. He also organised a blood transfusion service for the Middle East forces and pioneered the preferential use of whole blood for transfusion in casualties with severe blood loss. Also appointed Deputy Director of Pathology in the Middle East, he established forty laboratories and collaborated with Fairley in the control of malaria. Later he organised laboratory and blood transfusion services for the Normandy landings. After the war he was appointed Director of the celebrated Wellcome Laboratories of Tropical Medicine.

The Blitz produced its own 'new disease' – crush syndrome – kidney failure due to release of the protein myoglobin into the blood stream from damaged muscle tissue, occurring when people were trapped under falling masonry. Eric Bywaters (1910–2003; FRCP 1950), at the British Postgraduate Medical School in Hammersmith, discovered that administering alkaline solutions could keep patients alive and buy time for the kidneys to heal. The realisation that acute kidney failure could be recovered from if the patient survived long enough was a key medical discovery of the twentieth century. Bywaters also introduced the artificial kidney into the UK, by the generosity of Willem Kolff, who donated one of the first six artificial kidneys he had made, following his experiments in wartime Holland using sausage skins as a dialysis membrane and a rotatable drum derived from washing machine parts.

ABOVE: Willem Kolff's pioneer kidney dialysis machines (Reprinted by permission from Macmillan Publishers Ltd: The artificial kidney and its effect on the development of other artificial organs, Fig 1. *Nature Medicine.* Copyright 2002 Nature Publishing Group.)
RIGHT: Bywaters' and Beall's paper on crush injury and kidney function in the *British Medical Journal,* 1941 (Reprinted with permission. © 1941. BMJ. All rights reserved.)

The realisation that acute kidney failure could be recovered from if the patient survived long enough was a key medical discovery of the twentieth century.

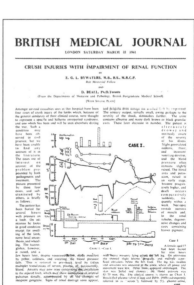

Finally, the emergence of rehabilitation medicine should be mentioned – to an extent another brainchild of George Riddoch. In World War I, Riddoch had had great experience of spinal injury, supervising cases evacuated from the battlefield to the Empire Hospital in London. Many men died from bladder infections and the few who survived were 'left on the scrap heap'. In World War II he worked to do better. Under his leadership, twelve specialised spinal units were set up, the first four being in Oswestry, Stanmore, Warrington and Bangor with a total of around 700 casualties treated. He wrote the Nerve Injuries Committee memorandum concerning spinal injury which covered topics such as the avoidance of plaster beds, bladder management with intermittent catheterisation as opposed to supra-pubic drainage, wash-outs, tidal drainage, the risks of infection, and also ways of avoiding pressure sores: much of his work still applies today. Riddoch travelled around the country visiting the units and giving advice and instruction. He was an inspiring teacher and without his personal oversight, conditions tended to deteriorate. His standards were extremely high, his workload prodigious, and his instructions were delivered always with courtesy and humour.

One of Riddoch's legacies was the visionary appointment of (Sir) Ludwig Guttmann (1899–1980; FRCP 1962) to take charge of the new spinal injuries unit at Stoke Mandeville (UK) in 1944. Guttmann had escaped from Nazi Germany in 1939 and, working in Oxford, he continued his physiological work on the effects of spinal injury on sweating ('sweaty Guttmann' as he was known by the many who did not like him). At Stoke Mandeville, Guttmann set about changing almost every concept of care. He supervised management personally around the clock and insisted on the highest standards. Patients were turned every two hours, their bladders dealt with, spinal surgery was advised against in most instances, and Guttmann sought to engage all with physiotherapy and with psychological and social rehabilitation. The emphasis on the latter resulted in the idea of introducing paraplegic sports in 1945. Sixteen ex-service patients competed in the first Stoke Mandeville International Wheelchair Games for the paraplegic in 1948 and in 1952 he persuaded the Dutch to send a team. He invented the term 'paralympics' and his efforts led to the first Olympic Games for the paralysed in Rome in 1960. Despite his overbearing and intolerant demeanour, more than any other doctor before him, Guttmann improved the lot of the war-wounded and the physically disabled. John Silver (FRCP 1963) records how Guttmann could transform the life of a paralysed person 'covered in pressure sores; his kidneys … full of stones … and practically dead', but only by being bloody minded, often overbearing and at times quite intolerable. When Silver took over the directorship of Stoke Mandeville, he learned that leadership can usefully involve 'persuasion and consensus rather than fear, intrigue and intimidation'.

In World War II, four fellows, eighteen members and 243 licentiates lost their lives (of the about 2,500 fellows and members, and 580 new licentiates in 1945).

POSTSCRIPT

Lord Russell Brain's diaries mused that World War I would end militarism, 'for the men who have been into battle will never believe a militarist again … '. That was a hope too far, an illusion abruptly ended in 1939, and five years after the end of World War II Britain was again fighting, this time against communists in Korea. Additionally, the Cold War between the West and the Soviet Union was fuelling an escalation of militarism and armament.

On 20 January 1951, at the height of the Korean War, seven doctors, five of whom were fellows of the College, published a letter in *The Lancet* expressing concern about the arms race, the impact of arms spending on healthcare ('each pound spent on bombs means … more dead babies now') and the apathetic drift towards another world war.

> We appeal to all our fellow doctors who think there may yet be an alternative to merely providing treatment for casualties ; we ask them to join us, in the spirit of our chosen profession of healing, in doing all in their power to halt preparation for war and to bring about a new and determined approach to the peaceful settlement of disputes and to world disarmament.
>
> RICHARD DOLL   HORACE JOULES
> ALFRED ESTERMAN   DUNCAN LEYS
> IAN GILLILAND   MARTIN POLLOCK
>   LIONEL PENROSE.
> 24, Lansdowne Road,
> London, W.11.

The letter provoked many responses, to *The Lancet* and privately. Not all agreed with its perspective. Some respondents had argued that war and peace were political matters which should not be discussed in a medical journal. The seven profoundly disagreed:

Doctors have a social responsibility as well as a personal one to their patients; they have an ethical tradition and an international allegiance. War is a symptom of mental ill health. Its results include wounds and disease. Doctors are therefore properly concerned in preventing it.

MEDICAL ASSOCIATION FOR
PREVENTION OF WAR

AND IT GOES ON . . .

Years during which British forces have not been involved in military conflicts somewhere are rare – certainly there have been none since 1914. Innovation in physicianly practice, which as noted before made little impact in war prior to the beginning of the twentieth century, has continued, not only in bringing advanced medical care to the battlefront but also, for example, in demonstrating the efficacy of newer approaches to resuscitation and preparation for surgery. One of the innovators in the field is Brigadier Tim Hodgetts (1963– ; FRCP 1999), at the time of writing Medical Director in the Defence Medical Services, who became brusquely alerted to the importance of improvised and rapid responses to emergencies in 1991

Subsequently, a meeting in London, attended by 130 doctors, led to the founding of the Medical Association for the Prevention of War (MAPW). The authors of the letter to *The Lancet* included Sir Richard Doll (1912–2005; FRCP 1937; FRS), world famous for establishing the link between smoking and medicine, who had served in France as a battalion medical officer and then on a hospital ship near Cairo; and Lionel Penrose (1898–1972; FRCP 1962; FRS), one of the world's foremost human geneticists who had served in France in the Friend's Ambulance Brigade in 1918.

The MAPW provoked dissent – denounced as communist – and its opposition to the nuclear deterrent was far from popular. It later affiliated with the International Physicians for the Prevention of Nuclear War (IPPNW, Nobel Peace Prize Winner in 1985) and in the UK eventually merged with the Medical Campaign against Nuclear Weapons to form Medical Action for Global Security, a 'health professionals' organisation challenging barriers to health' such as violent conflict and poverty.

TOP: Cover design for the journal of the Medical Association for the Prevention of War, 1983 (© University of Bradford Special Collections)
RIGHT: Brigadier Tim Hodgetts (© Tim Hodgetts)

ABOVE: Troops carry a wounded comrade to a Blackhawk medivac helicopter. Corporal Dan Bardsley RLC (Crown Copyright 2016)
PAGES OVERLEAF: 'F' force survivors from the Death Railway. The medium was brass polish and medicine sediment on paper (Charles Thrale 1943)

when a Semtex bomb exploded and destroyed the emergency department at Musgrave Park Hospital in Belfast where he was working. Further active service in Kosovo, Iraq and Afghanistan saw the progressive upgrading of front-line services and equipment in armoured field ambulances and the approach of direct leadership of medical services in the battlefront. 'The life of a consultant in emergency medicine … is no more important or vital than the life of a private soldier'. The ability to resuscitate, intubate, insert chest drains and transfuse on the floor of a military helicopter has enhanced the survivability of severe military injuries, though they bring with it the problems faced in rehabilitation of 'unexpected survivors', left with disabilities which formerly would have been prevented by death.

Finally to Bill Frankland (1912– ; FRCP 1995, President's Medal 2015), at the time of writing 103 years old, the most senior fellow of the College. As he wrote: 'I've been so near death so many times'. At the fall of Singapore, in 1942, he was captured by the Japanese and remained a prisoner of war for two and a half years. As a doctor in the camps, he encountered terrible disease, pain and death. He was subjected to appalling abuse, illness, repeated brutal beatings and severe privation. He survived, whereas many did not, and went on to have a distinguished career in medicine in the field of immunology. He retains an infectious sense of enjoyment of life, humour and tremendous verve. He represents the real spirit of physicians and of the College; it is fitting to end this little volume with grateful reflection on his sense of duty and humanity.

FURTHER READING

Here are a selection of books, journal articles and other sources which cover topics touched upon in the text, and from some of which quotations are taken. This is not a comprehensive reference list, but should give the reader an introduction to the large literature on this topic.

Anon. *Mr Churchill with the Physicians.* British Medical Journal 1944 (March 11) i: 368

Anon. *The Women of Royaumont.* http://historycompany.co.uk/2011/11/29/the-women-of-royaumont-a-unique-film/

Anon. *Report of the War Office Committee of Enquiry into 'Shell Shock.'* (The Southborough Committee) HMSO: London, 1922

Blair J. *Centenary History of the Royal Army Medical Corp1898–1998.* Scottish Academic Press, Edinburgh; 1998

Blanco R.L. *Wellington's Surgeon General: Sir James McGrigor.* Duke University Press: Durham, 1974

Bliss M. *Harvey Cushing: A life in Surgery.* University of Toronto Press: Toronto, 2005

Briggs A. *A History of the Royal College of Physicians* Vol 4. Oxford University Press: Oxford, 2005

Clark G. *A History of the Royal College of Physicians* Vols 1 and 2. Oxford University Press: Oxford, 1964 and 1966

Cohen S. *Medical Services in the First World War.* Shire: Oxford, 2014

Cooke A.M. *A History of the Royal College of Physicians* Vol 3. Oxford University Press: Oxford, 1972

Cope Z. *Florence Nightingale and the Doctors,* The Museum Press: London, 1958

Crew F.A. *Official History of the Second World War. Army Medical Services.* HMSO: London, 1956

Crumplin M. *Guthrie's War: A Surgeon of the Peninsula and Waterloo.* Pen and Sward Military: Barnsley, 2010

Crumplin M. *Men of Steel; Surgery in the Napoleonic Wars.* Quiller Press: Shrewsbury, 2007

Davenport G. (ed). *The Royal College of Physicians and its collections: An Illustrated History.* James & James: London, 2001

Fitzgerald G. *Chemical Warfare and the Medical Response During World War I.* Am J Public Health 2008; 98: 611–625

Florey H.W. and Cairns H. *Investigation of War Wounds. Penicillin: A preliminary report to the War Office and the Medical Research Council on investigations concerning the use of penicillin in war wounds* (War Office A.M.D. 7 October). London, 1948

Fulton J. *Harvey Cushing: A biography.* Charles C. Thomas: Springfield, 1948

Goss B.C. *An Artillery Gas Attack.* Journal of industrial and engineering chemistry 1919; 11: 829–836

Harrison M. *The Medical War: British Military Medicine in the First World War.* Oxford University Press: Oxford, 2010

Herringham W. *A Physician in France.* Edward Arnold: London, 1919

Herringham W. *Medical Services, Diseases of the War.* In the History of the Great War. HMSO: London, 1922

Hudson G.L. *British Military and Naval Medicine.* Clio Medica 2007; 81:7–22

Howard M. *Wellington's Doctors: British Army Medical Services in the Napoleonic Wars.* Spellmount: Staplehurst, 2002

Howell H.A.L. *The British Medical Arrangements during the Waterloo Campaign.* Proc R Soc Med. 1924; 17(Sect Hist Med): 39–50

Keevil J.J. *Medicine and the Navy,* Vols 1 & 2. E & S Livingstone: Edinburgh, 1957

Kempthorne G.A. *The Waterloo campaign.* J R Army Med Corps 1933; 60: 52–58

Linden S, Jones E. *Shell Shock Revisited: An Examination of the Records of the National Hospital in London.* Med Hist 2014; 58: 519–545

Lovell R. *Churchill's Doctor: A Biography of Lord Moran.* Parthenon: New York, 1993

Macpherson W.G. *History of the Great War based on official documents by direction of the Historical Section of the Committee of Imperial Defence. Medical Services: General History* Vol. 1. Macmillan: London, 1921

Macpherson W.G. *History of the Great War based on official documents by direction of the Historical Section of the Committee of Imperial Defence. Medical Services: General History* Vol. 2 Macmillan: London, 1923

Matthew C. (ed). *Oxford Dictionary of National Biography.* Oxford University Press: Oxford, 2004

McGuffie T.H. *The Walcheren Expedition and the Walcheren Fever. The English Historical Review,* 1947; 62 (no. 243): 191–202

Maurin M. and Raoult D. *Bartonella (Rochalimaea) Quintana Infections.* Clinical Microbiological Review 1996; 9:273–292

Myers C.S. *A Contribution to the Study of Shell Shock. The Lancet,* 1915; 185 (4772): 316–320

Nichol J. and Rennel T. *MEDIC: Saving Lives from Dunkirk to Afghanistan.* Penguin: New York, 2009

Shepherd J. *The Crimean Doctors.* Liverpool University Press: Liverpool, 1991

Shipp J. *Memoirs of the Extraordinary Military Career of John Shipp, late a lieut. in His Majesty's 87th regiment.* Fisher Unwin: London, 1890

Silver J. *George Riddoch: The Man who Found Ludwig Guttmann.* Spinal Cord 2012; 50: 88–93

Turner W.A. *The Bradshaw Lecture on Neuroses and Psychoses of War. The Lancet* 1918 192, (4967): 613–17

Various Authors. *Biographical Memoirs of Fellows of the Royal Society. Royal Society of Medicine.* 1955 onwards; *Philosophical transactions of the Royal Society. Series B.* 1896 onwards

Various Authors. Scarlet Finders. http://www.scarletfinders.co.uk

Waddington I. *The Struggle to Reform the Royal College of Physicians, 1767–1771.* Journal of Medical History 1973; 17: 107–121

Walker A.L. *A Base Hospital in France.* Scarlet Finders. http://www.scarletfinders.co.uk/156.html

Wilson C. *The Anatomy of Courage.* Constable: London, 1945

Yealland L.R. *Hysterical Disorders of Warfare.* London: MacMillan, 1918

ARCHIVE COLLECTIONS

Archives of the Royal College of Physicians, London
https://www.rcplondon.ac.uk/archive-and-historical-library-collections

Archives of the Wellcome Library
http://wellcomelibrary.org/collections/about-the-collections/archives-and-manuscripts/

Archives of the Imperial War Museum
http://www.iwm.org.uk/collections

Munk's Roll (Lives of the Fellows). A collection of obituaries of almost all fellows and licentiates of the Royal College of Physicians since its foundation in 1518 – grouped into 12 volumes, and all available online at: http://munksroll.rcplondon.ac.uk

Friends' ambulance train at Amiens. Lionel Penrose 1918, while serving in Friends' Ambulance Brigade (Courtesy of Professor Shirley Hodgson)